COLOSSIANS

A SHORT EXEGETICAL
AND PASTORAL COMMENTARY

Colossians

A SHORT
EXEGETICAL AND PASTORAL
COMMENTARY

Anthony C. Thiselton

 CASCADE *Books* · Eugene, Oregon

COLOSSIANS
A Short Exegetical and Pastoral Commentary

Cascade Books
An Imprint of Wipf and Stock Publishers
199 W. 8th Ave., Suite 3
Eugene, OR 97401

www.wipfandstock.com

PAPERBACK ISBN: 978-1-7252-5852-5
HARDCOVER ISBN: 978-1-7252-5853-2
EBOOK ISBN: 978-1-7252-5854-9

Cataloguing-in-Publication data:

Names: Thiselton, Anthony C., author.

Title: Colossians: a short exegetical and pastoral commentary / Anthony C. Thiselton.

Description: Eugene, OR : Cascade Books, 2020 | Includes bibliographical references and index.

Identifiers: ISBN 978-1-7252-5852-5 (paperback) | ISBN 978-1-7252-5853-2 (hardcover) | ISBN 978-1-7252-5854-9 (ebook)

Subjects: LCSH: Bible—Colossians—Commentaries.

Classification: LCC BS2715.3 T44 2020 (print) | BS2715.3 (ebook)

Manufactured in the U.S.A.   MAY 7, 2020

Contents

Contents

Abbreviations

AV/KJB	Authorized Version of the Bible/King James' Bible
BDAG	F. W. Danker, *A Greek-English Lexicon of the New Testament and Other Early Christian Literature* (3rd ed. Chicago: Chicago University Press, 2000; based on the Lexicon by W. Bauer, W. F. Arndt and F. W. Gingrich)
CGTC	Cambridge Greek Testament Commentary
ECNT	Zondervan Exegetical Commentary on the New Testament
GNB	Good News Bible (Today's English Version)
ICC	International Critical Commentary
JSNTS	Journal for the Study of the New Testament Supplement
NASB	New American Standard Bible
NIB	The New Interpreter's Bible (Nashville: Abingdon, 2000)
NICNT	The New International Commentary on the New Testament
NIGTC	The New International Greek Testament Commentary
NIV	New International Version
NLC	New London Commentary

NJB	New Jerusalem Bible
NPNF	The Nicene and Post-Nicene Fathers
NRSV	New Revised Standard Version
PNTC	Pillar New Testament Commentary
TCNT	Twentieth Century New Testament
TDNT	*Theological Dictionary of the New Testament*, edited by By G. Kittel and G. Friedrich (ET, Grand Rapids: Eerdmans, 10 vols., 1964–76)
THNTC	Two Horizons New Testament Commentary
TNTC	Tyndale New Testament Commentary
UBS	United Bible Societies
WBC	Word Biblical Commentary
WUNT	Wissenschaftliche Untersuchungen zum Neuen Testament

Preface

I SHOULD LIKE TO make three points. First, I have tried to model this commentary on last year's book, *2 Corinthians: A Short Exegetical and Pastoral Commentary* (Eugene, Oregon: Wipf and Stock, Cascade Books, 2019).

Second, unlike the earlier book, I have attempted a new translation of the Greek text. This is not because I am dissatisfied with all earlier English translations, but because I have been able to benefit from the insights of Frederick Danker, Murray Harris, A. T. Robertson, and many others.

Third, I should like to express my gratitude to Rev. Dr. Robin Parry, Wipf and Stock's editor in England, for numerous improvements, advice, and suggestions, concerning the manuscript. I am also grateful to Heather Carraher for her careful preparation of the printed text in the U.S.A., and to my wife, Rosemary, for her constant support through fifty-seven years,

Anthony C. Thiselton, FBA, May 2020

Part I

INTRODUCTION

Introduction

A. The Church at Colossae

Colossae was a city of Phrygia, about 150 miles to the east of Ephesus, thirteen miles to the northeast of Hierapolis, and ten or eleven miles to the west of Laodicea. The city was in the Southern part of the Roman Province of Asia, or in modern Turkey. Colossae was once a city of great importance and wealth but was overtaken in size by Hierapolis and Laodicea. The earlier wealth of Colossae four or five centuries previous was due to its position on the main road from Ephesus and Sardis to the Euphrates and to its wool industry.[1] All three cities were situated in the valley of the River Lycus, a tributary of the river Meander. Colossae would

1. Lohse, *Colossians and Philemon*, 20.

have benefitted from the stream of travelers who brought news and currents of thought to the Lycus Valley from afar. Laodicea became the financial and administrative center of the three cities. Meanwhile Hierapolis attracted many visitors because of its hot mineral springs. However, by Paul's time Strabo and Pliny described Colossae as a small town.[2] Philo and Josephus indicate that there were Jewish colonies in these cities of Phrygia, although the church of Colossae was predominantly gentile when Paul wrote. Colossae, though small, was relatively prosperous, exporting wool and a highly prized purple dye.

Although he preached in Phrygia, we have no record that Paul ever visited Colossae, though it is possible that he passed through the city without pausing to preach. According to Acts 19:10, Paul made Ephesus his center for operations for two years. His letter to the believers in Colossae was prompted when he received a report of the church from Epaphras, probably when Paul was under guard or in prison in Rome. Epaphras was probably the founder of the Colossian church (Col 1:6–7), perhaps around about the mid-50s. We need not imagine that Paul's audience was a single gathering of Christians for there may have been more than one house church in Colossae.

What concerned Paul enough to write to a church that he himself had not founded? A. S. Peake writes, "Recently they [the Colossians] had been assailed by a form of false teaching, and while they remained, so far, loyal to the doctrine they had been taught (1:4; 2:5), the danger was sufficiently serious to call forth this letter."[3]

B. The False Teaching, Formerly Called "The Colossian Heresy"

Dunn writes, "There has been a long tradition of speaking of 'the Colossians heresy' or 'false teaching' as that which Paul sought to

---

2. Lightfoot, *St Paul's Epistles to the Colossians and to Philemon*, 16, n.1.

3. Peake, "Colossians," 478.

attack and refute, a tradition that continues to the present. The language is potentially misleading."[4] He argues this on two grounds. First, there was once a clear conception of what Christian orthodoxy embodied with clearly delineated boundaries which marked off "Christianity" from other religious groupings. He argues, "such a view can no longer be sustained, at least in that simple form."[5] Dunn claims that earliest Christianity itself contained a large measure of diversity. He has written extensively on this theme.[6] Dunn's position is understandable in the light of subsequent over-tight notions of orthodoxy. However, departures from Pauline Christianity clearly characterize Paul's opponents in Colossae. We can avoid the term "heresy" without losing Paul's concern for right or correct Christology.

Second, Dunn argues that according to the older view the church was in crisis because a vigorous group of teachers in Colossae were attempting to subvert the gospel preached by Paul and the Pauline circle. This crisis allegedly mirrored the kind of confrontation that existed between Paul and false teachers in Galatians. By contrast, the more modern view emphasizes that there is nothing in Colossians like the fierceness and explicitness of the denunciations that feature in Galatians (Gal 1:6–9; 3:1–3; 4:8–10; 5:2–12). "By contrast," writes Dunn, "the mood in Colossians is surprisingly relaxed: a lengthy development section (1:9—2:7) before the first clear warning notes are sounded (2:8); a central section with firm rebuttal and relatively restrained polemic limited to 2:16–23; and a still longer concluding section with extensive parenesis, again giving no clear evidence of false teaching being counted."[7] Dunn, like many others, appeals to a 1973 article by Morna Hooker to substantiate this claim.[8] Once again, the argument is correct, but must not be overemphasized. Paul clearly regarded false teaching

---

4. Dunn, *Colossians and Philemon*, 24.

5. Dunn, *Colossians and Philemon*, 24.

6. Dunn, *Unity and Diversity in the New Testament*.

7. Dunn, *Colossians and Philemon*, 26.

8. Hooker, "Were There False Teachers in Colossae?"

as a threat to the church. The argument is perhaps largely a matter of perception and nomenclature.

The so-called false teachers called their system a "philosophy" (2:8). It concerned "wisdom" (1:9, 28; 2:3, 23; 3:16; 4:5), "knowledge" (1:6, 9–10; 2:2–3; 3:10), and "elements of the universe" (Gk, *ta stoicheia tou kosmou*; 2:8, 20). These are associated with "angels" (2:18) and "cosmic powers" (2:10, 15), and perhaps "fullness" (2:9, 10). If this is in the tradition of later gnostic thought, the key for young Christians would be whether reliance upon these would guarantee "entrance" into a fuller salvation. With these concepts Paul brackets subservience to regulations and ascetical practice (2:16, 21, 23). By contrast with this philosophy and its accompanying praxis, Paul underlines the all-sufficiency of Jesus Christ for full salvation: *Christ is everything that the Colossians need.* It is unnecessary to assume that the false teaching amounted to a system; more probably it involved syncretic elements from proto-Gnosticism and possibly the mystery religions.[9]

At the same time we should not ignore the distinctively Jewish features that characterize gnostic threats. Clearly there were Jewish ethnic minorities in the cities of the Lycus Valley. In 2:11 and 13 Paul alludes to a circumcision "not made with hands," and the Dead Sea Scrolls refer to ascetic practices. We have evidence of Judaism being combined with elements of Gnosticism and a primitive form of this may be what we find behind the "philosophy" Paul confronts in Colossians.

The attempt to reconstruct the false teaching is so complex that we may repeat Andrew Lincoln's conclusion: "The very number and variety of proposed solutions to the identity of the philosophy should caution against any overtly confident claims to reconstruct it."[10]

9. See Bornkamm, "The Heresy of Colossians."

10. Lincoln, *Colossians*, 561.

C. Questions about the Authorship of Colossians

Most of the arguments against Paul's authorship of Colossians date from the time of E. T. Mayerhoff in 1838. He regarded this epistle to be dependent on Ephesians, which he did not regard as Pauline. Objections to Paul's authorship depend on the theology of Colossians, as well as its vocabulary and style. In terms of the latter, there are thirty-three *hapax legomena* (words peculiar to Colossians in the New Testament), the heaping up of synonyms (such as praying and asking, or spiritual wisdom and understanding), and genitival connectives. Many writers claim that the style is cumbersome, verbose, with a maximum of subordinate clauses with participles and infinitives rather than finite verbs. Anyone who reads the Greek will readily agree with this analysis. In terms of *theological* objections to Pauline authorship, supposedly characteristic Pauline themes seem to be missing, such as righteousness, justification, the law, salvation, and revelation.

Many of the questions about vocabulary and style, however, can be answered by pointing to the freedom accorded to secretaries. Recently E. Randolph Richards has demonstrated Paul's use of such resources.[11] It may have been the secretary or amanuensis who introduced these stylistic peculiarities. This is especially likely if Paul was detained in some kind of protective custody or custody pending trial. Further, much of the choice of vocabulary may well have been determined by the nature of the false teaching that the author wishes to correct.

Werner Kümmel adds a corrective: "On the other hand Colossians shows clear stylistic peculiarities of Paul."[12] He gives the examples in Paul's Greek that find parallels in Colossians: (a) *kai* (and) after *dia touto* (on account of this) (Col 1:9; cf. 1 Thess 2:13; 3:5; Rom 13:6); (b) *hoi hagioi autou*, the/his saints (Col 1:26; cf. 1 Thess 3:13; 2 Thess 1:10); (c) *charizesthai* in the sense of forgive (Col 2:13; 3:13; cf. 2 Cor 2:7, 10; 12:13); (d) *en merei* in the sense

11. Richards, *Paul and First-Century Letter Writing*, especially 81–93; and Richards, *The Secretary in the Letters of Paul*.

12. Kümmel, *Introduction to the New Testament*, 241.

of "with regard to" (Col 2:16; cf. 2 Cor 3:10; 9:3); (e) and *pan ergon agathon*, every good work, (Col 1:10; cf. 2 Cor 9:8; 2 Thess 2:17). He concludes, "The language and style of Colossians, therefore, gives no cause to doubt the Pauline origin of the epistle."[13]

If we select two more recent writers who express doubts about the Pauline authorship, we find that theology rather than style is regarded as the decisive factor. Lincoln acknowledges that the use of widespread use of secretaries or amanuenses could account for unexpected stylistic phenomena. The main argument, he recognizes, depends on the theology that we find.[14] The linguistic objections are thus not enough to rule out Paul as the author.

James Dunn is similarly hesitant to exclude outright the possibility of Pauline authorship, but he asserts, "It is difficult to deny that the theological parenetic content is significantly different from what we are accustomed to in all the undisputed Paulines."[15] He points especially to the Christology in Col 1:15–20 and 2:9–10, although he also admits that similarities can be found in 1 Cor 8:6 and Phil 2:6–11. Elsewhere he says, "It [the epistle] serves as a bridge between the undisputed Paulines and those members of the Pauline corpus that are generally considered post-Pauline."[16] In other words, Colossians belongs to the broader Pauline corpus, but doubts about Paul's authorship on balance point to a post-Pauline author. This is mainly on the grounds of a more developed theology than we might expect from Paul himself. More recently still, Robert Wilson sympathizes with Dunn's view after an extensive discussion of pseudepigraphy and the possibility of Paul's authorship.[17]

Yet several more recent writers still support the traditional view that Paul himself wrote Colossians. Douglas Moo first dismisses issues about style and vocabulary on the ground that writers frequently use secretaries or an amanuensis, and then refers

13. Kümmel, *Introduction to the New Testament*, 241.

14. Lincoln, *Colossians*, 577.

15. Dunn, *Colossians and Philemon*, 36.

16. Dunn, *Colossians and Philemon*, 19.

17. Wilson, *Colossians and Philemon*, 9–19.

to Paul's characteristic emphasis on received tradition (Col 2:8; 1 Cor 15:1–3) and the universality of his apostleship.[18] Although Colossians' Christology is exceptional, parallels can be found in the undisputed Pauline epistles (1 Cor 8:6; Phil 2:5–11; 1 Cor 1:18, 24).[19] In the most basic terms, Colossians does not contradict Paul. Moo concludes, "We are not at all convinced, then, that Colossians stands in theological contrast with the other Pauline letters in the four areas usually mentioned."[20] Further, after a discussion of pseudepigraphy, he also concludes that pseudepigraphical theories of the authorship of Colossians must be rejected.[21]

A second recent defender of the traditional view of Paul's authorship is Scot McKnight.[22] He appreciates the complexity of the problem of speaking of the authentic Paul, and expresses sympathy with the careful approach of Dunn, especially "given what we know today about how letters were produced."[23] He warns us that there is simply not enough evidence to know what many think they know. This especially applies to issues of style and perhaps vocabulary. George Cannon, he points out, showed how instances of supposed tensions turn out to be Paul using existing traditions.[24] McKnight in the end defends the Pauline authorship, not because he feels obliged to do so, but because "My contention is not with the unknown side but with the known side."[25] In other words, he offers two reasons why he defends the Pauline authorship: first, he feels no external pressure to do so, apart from his own inner conviction; second, in assessing both sides of the debate, he has come to believe that those who support Paul's authorship can rely on the early testimony of the church, while those who deny Paul's

---

18. Moo, *The Letters to the Colossians and to Philemon*, 32–33.

19. Moo, *The Letters to the Colossians and to Philemon*, 34–35.

20. Moo, *The Letters to the Colossians and to Philemon*, 36.

21. Moo, *The Letters to the Colossians and to Philemon*, 37–41.

22. McKnight, *The Letter to the Colossians*, 5–18.

23. McKnight, *The Letter to the Colossians*, 8.

24. McKnight, *The Letter to the Colossians*, 9; Cannon, *The Use of Traditional Materials in Colossians*.

25. McKnight, *The Letter to the Colossians*, 10.

authorship are forced to rely of a multitude of sheer speculations. A third modern defender of the Pauline authorship is David Pao, mainly on the grounds of Colossians' similarities with Philemon and Philippians.[26]

The theological objections to Pauline authorship are more precarious than many suppose. F. C. Baur may have over-influenced too many scholars in thinking that the authentic Paul could only repeat what he wrote in the four major epistles. This may narrow Paul's vision more than was legitimate, for Baur offers a speculative and circular argument. Werner Kümmel declared in 1965, "The absence of well-known Pauline concepts proves nothing, because analogous observations can also be made about other Pauline epistles [with undisputed authorship]."[27] Thankfully, scholars have partly progressed beyond Baur's narrow focus in the move to argue that Paul is not to be restricted to the thought of a so-called "Lutheran" Paul. In spite of possible overstatement, E. P. Sanders pointed the way forward in his *Paul and Palestinian Judaism*.[28] To say this is not to endorse uncritically the "new" look on Paul, but it is to recognize the advance that we are indicating. And it opens us up to imagine a Paul with a wider theological range than Baur allowed for.

Additionally, the notion that Paul's theology did not develop beyond that of the more major epistles is at best strange. We may easily imagine that the apostle was thankful that controversies about justification by grace alone and issues about the law had been adequately addressed in Galatians, Romans, and 1 and 2 Corinthians, and that now other areas of thought and doctrine needed further attention. Christology and ecclesiology would be prime candidates. Christology had not been a divisive issue in the era of Galatians and Romans, but that situation has changed. Might not Paul have wished to develop the Christology he had already indicated in 1 Cor 8:6 and Phil 2:5–11 to respond to the new situation

26. David W. Pao, *Colossians and Philemon* (ECNew Testament; Grand Rapids: Zondervan, 2012) 20–23.

27. Kümmel, *Introduction to the New Testament*, 241.

28. Sanders, *Paul and Palestinian Judaism* (1977).

arising in Colossae? This is all the more plausible if Paul drew here on common pre-Pauline formulations. The Gospel traditions might have focused too much upon the pre-Easter Jesus, and Paul (like John) might have been discontented with this emphasis. The emergence of the false teaching that faced the Colossians would have made such development more urgent.

The classic case for the defense of Paul's authorship has been set out by F. F. Bruce, R. P. Martin, Peter T. O'Brien and N. T. Wright (as well as by McKnight, Pao, and Moo, discussed above).[29] O'Brien writes, "The tradition that Colossians is a genuine Pauline epistle stands on good ground."[30] Hardly any scholar nowadays, except F. C. Synge, believes that Colossians is dependent on Ephesians, as E. T. Mayerhoff had suggested. If there is dependence, it is the reverse way round.[31] Even those who—like Lohse, MacDonald, Dunn, and Lincoln—in the end doubt the Pauline authorship conclude that arguments about style and language cannot be decisive.[32] Everything hinges on the alleged non-Pauline theology. Thus, Wright concludes, "The real weight of the argument against Pauline authorship lies, I believe, on the question of theology."[33] He adds, "The theology of Colossians does not evidence a uniformly 'late' view, but links itself to major themes in all of Paul's other letters. The Christology fits well with Phil. 2:5–11 and 1 Cor. 8:6. . . . There is therefore no need to reject the Pauline authorship of Colossians."[34]

29. O'Brien, *Colossians, Philemon*, xli–xlix; Wright, *Colossians and Philemon*, 33–37; Martin, *Colossians and Philemon*, 32–40; and Bruce and Simpson, *The Epistles of Paul to the Ephesians and Colossians*, 170–73.

30. O'Brien, *Colossians, Philemon*, xli.

31. See J. B. Polhill's thorough survey of the relation between Ephesians and Colossians in "The Relationship between Ephesians and Colossians," 439–50.

32. Lohse, *Colossians and Philemon*, 4; Lohse, "Christusherrschaft und Kirche im Kolosserbrief"; MacDonald, *Colossians, Ephesians*, 6–9.

33. Wright, *Colossians and Philemon*, 35.

34. Wright, *Colossians and Philemon*, 36.

D. The Place of Writing of the Epistle and Its Probable Date

Paul alludes to his imprisonment in 4:3. The letter is also often linked with Philemon, Ephesians (Eph 6:20), and Philippians (Phil 1:12–30), which are known as the letters from prison. There were three possible periods when Paul may have been imprisoned, depending on the place of his imprisonment. 1 Corinthians 1:8 and 15:52 refer to *Ephesus;* Acts 24:27 refers to *Caesarea;* Acts 28:16ff. refers to *Rome.* There are further allusions to Paul's imprisonments in 2 Cor 6:5 and 11:23. Different scholars have argued for each of these places for Paul's imprisonment when he wrote Colossians. In some cases the same data can point to more than one possible place and date. For example, references to the praetorian guard and to Caesar's household (Phil 1:13 and 4:22) could indicate Rome or Ephesus or Caesarea. Wright and others suggest that each place is "Incapable of cast-iron proof."[35]

Until relatively recent times the scholarly consensus was that Paul was kept in some kind of custody in Rome. Eusebius records that Paul had a measure of freedom in Rome, which would account for the presence of co-workers and friends (Col 4:7–17). Some could engage in letter-writing for Paul. It can be argued that the runaway slave Onesimus could seek anonymity in the Imperial city. Rome is clearly the favored candidate on the basis of Acts, although Acts 24:27 speaks of two years imprisonment in Caesarea. O'Brien argues that on the basis of Acts alone, "No other imprisonment in Acts [than Rome] seems a real alternative."[36] Bruce and Moule tend to agree. An imprisonment in Ephesus would suggest a date of around 54–57, but Rome would allow a later date. Bruce asserts, "It is difficult to date it [Colossians] during his Ephesian ministry."[37] Rome is preferred "on all counts." Martin warns us "that speculations based on reconstructions of later developments

---

35. Wright, *Colossians and Philemon*, 38.
36. O'Brien, *Colossians, Philemon*, l.
37. Bruce, *Ephesians, Colossians*, 411–12.

in Paul's missionary strategy are too uncertain to opt firmly for an alternative to Rome."[38]

There are some factors which argue against Rome. One is the distance from Rome to Colossae, which is about 1,200 miles. Epaphras and Onesimus have already come to Paul; Tychicus and Onesimus are also to return. Paul's hopes to visit Colossae (Phlm 22) seem to clash with his plans to visit Spain (Rom 15:28). George Ogg explores these issues.[39]

Nevertheless, the case against Caesarea or Ephesus as Paul's place of imprisonment faces greater difficulties. Caesarea seems a relatively small town to become the base for Paul's later missionary activity.[40] Advocates of Ephesus as the place of Paul's imprisonment include Adolf Deissmann and George Duncan.[41] Duncan's thorough 300-page work reconstructs Paul's chronology in detail, including his relation to Onesimus and other figures, his use of Ephesus as a base for mission, his organization of the collection, and opposition to Paul. He sees Paul's imprisonment as a direct result of the Demetrius riot (Acts 19:23–41). Nevertheless, O'Brien represents a consensus when he concludes, "Of the three options, Ephesus and Rome have greater claims . . . than Caesarea. The Ephesian hypothesis has many strong points in its favor and cannot be entirely ruled out. . . . On balance we prefer this alternative [i.e., Rome]."[42] Wright endorses this conclusion, pointing out that all theories are no more than hypotheses.

Wright dates the epistle "between 52 and 55 (or possibly between 53 and 56)."[43] O'Brien proposes 60–61 on the assumption of imprisonment in Rome, and 54–57 on the assumption of

---

38. Martin, *Colossians and Philemon*, 25–26

39. For a detailed exploration of these issues, see Ogg, *The Chronology of the Life of Paul*, 178–93.

40. O'Brien, *Colossians, Philemon*, lii.

41. Duncan, *St. Paul's Ephesian Ministry*, especially 111–15, 144–61, and 270–97.

42. O'Brien, *Colossians, Philemon*, liii.

43. Wright, *Colossians and Philemon*, 39.

imprisonment in Ephesus.[44] Kümmel suggests a date between 58 and 60 if Paul was imprisoned in Rome, and between 56 and 58 if this was in Ephesus.[45] Harris proposes similar dating.[46] Pao suggests between 60 and 62; Moo, 60–61; and McKnight, like Wright, the mid 50s, "perhaps even 57."[47]

E. Paul's Most Distinctive Theme: The Supremacy of the Cosmic Christ

The most distinctive theological passages in Colossians come in 1:16–19 and 2:9. In 1:16 Paul says that all things were created in Christ, whether in heaven or on earth, whether visible or invisible, whether thrones or lordly powers, whether rulers or authorities; everything was created through him and everything exists with him as its goal. On him creation depends, and for him it was created. In 2:9 Paul asserts, "In him the fullness of deity lives in a bodily way." This explicates what John says in his Prologue: "In the beginning was the Word . . . and the Word was God . . . and the Word became flesh and lived among us, and we beheld his glory" (John 1:1, 14). Many modern writers agree that "Here Christ is set forth in a cosmic context."[48]

Paul exults in the supremacy and all-sufficiency of Jesus Christ. He is Lord before and over every rival source of lordship and authority, whether this be angels and mythic forces or the dominance of the Roman state. He is also *all-sufficient* for salvation, in contrast to rival systems that may have been proposed in Colossae. Whether or not 1:15–20 may echo a previous formulation, Paul makes it his own and amplifies it in chapter 2. He and John in the Fourth Gospel supplement the view of Jesus painted in the first three Gospels. Christ is supreme and all-sufficient, far

44. O'Brien, *Colossians, Philemon*, liv.

45. Kümmel, *Introduction to the New Testament*, 245.

46. Harris, *Colossians and Philemon*, 4.

47. McKnight, *Letter to the Colossians*, 39; Pao, *Colossians and Philemon*, 25; Moo, *Colossians and Philemon*, 46.

48. White, "Colossians," 217.

above any other power. The universe exists only for his sake. He is the focal point whereby all things make sense in a coherent pattern (1:17).

In due course Paul will expound the practical and ethical consequences of being a Christian in Christ. But first comes contemplation of the identity and reality of Christ. This is like John's Prologue. It sets the scene for all that follows. Once the cosmic Christ is in view, all the ethical and practical injunctions make sense. We can even see the deception of the false teaching that used to be called "the Colossian heresy." For although Paul does not rebuke the Colossian community but commends their faithfullness, nevertheless false teachers have entered the church and try to seduce the believers from their faith in Christ.

Dunn claims that the letter's Christology and ecclesiology "seems significantly developed beyond what we find in the undisputed Paulines."[49] As a statement of sheer fact, this is true. But it hardly affects the question of Pauline authorship unless we assume that neither Paul's Christology nor his ecclesiology could have developed further. Dunn regards this epistle as very close to the beginning "in a post-Pauline trajectory." But it is natural to imagine Paul in his later years of "imprisonment" reflecting in dialogue with such Christians as Epaphras, that more was to be said than hitherto on the sovereignty and all-sufficiency of Christ and on the importance of the Church. We can only speculate whether Ephesians, which is later, brings this later thought to a climax.

From this hymn (Col 1:15–20) Lohse comments, "The letter develops its message in which Christ is proclaimed as Lord over all the world. In him the whole fullness of deity dwells bodily (2:9); he is the head of all powers and principalities (2:10); he is the head of his body, the Church (1:18)."[50]

---

49. Dunn, *Colossians and Philemon*, 19.
50. Lohse, *Colossians and Philemon*, 3.

Part II

Exegesis

I

Introduction

1:1–14

1. Address and greeting (1:1–2)

1 Paul, an apostle of Christ Jesus through the will of God and Timothy his brother, **2** to the holy people and faithful brothers and sisters in Christ in Colossae, grace and peace to you from God our Father.[1]

It was conventional in ancient Greco-Roman letters to begin with the name of the writer or sender, followed by the name of the addressee. Although Paul had not personally visited Colossae, the Colossian Christians would have been familiar with the name of Paul, not least through his Ephesian ministry in c.52–55 A.D. (cf. Acts 19:10, 17–20, and 23–41). He wrote this letter because Epaphras had given him a report of the church. In 1:7 Paul refers to "Epaphras our beloved fellow servant." Paul is about to draw his readers' attention to the pre-eminence and all-sufficiency of Christ, and so he calls himself an apostle of Jesus Christ, as one who bears the commission of Christ to represent him. He thus

---

1. All translations are the author's own. Textual note: later MSS add "and from the Lord Jesus Christ."

states his credentials for writing to this church which he had not visited.

Jeffrey Crafton remarks that in Paul's view apostles become transparent windows through which people see God in Christ.[2] Chrysostom similarly points out that the title "apostle" is a humble word because it points away from the self to Christ.[3] In the Pauline writings, an "apostle" is a witness of Christ's resurrection. In Luke-Acts and the first three Gospels, by contrast, the term mainly refers to the twelve who followed Jesus during his earthly ministry. Crafton's comment harmonizes with Lightfoot's pronouncement that "by the will of God" is not polemical but should "be regarded as a renunciation of all personal worth, and a declaration of God's unmerited grace."[4] Calvin observes, "He [Paul] was not bound to one church merely, but his apostleship extended to all."[5]

In Colossians, Paul arguably does not need to claim a special authority for opposing many of the beliefs or practices of his readers. He describes them as "faithful brothers and sisters" (v. 2). Most modern writers argue that there is no evidence that Paul's authority has been challenged by the Colossians. On the other hand, Margaret MacDonald believes that Paul appeals to his apostleship because he has to contend with those who bring false teaching and compares Colossians with the situation in Galatians.[6] That is why, she says, he appeals to "the will of God," for this provides evidence for the supernatural element cited as requirement for "charismatic" leaders in the view of Max Weber, as well as requiring a network of collaborators.

Eduard Lohse acknowledges both points of view. He writes, "Although the community's life and conduct offer no cause for reprimand, the author of the letter is deeply worried that the community, unsuspecting and innocent as it is, may be led astray by false teaching and become the victim of deceivers." He continues, "For

2. Crafton, *The Agency of the Apostle*, especially 63–102.
3. Chrysostom, *Epistle to the Corinthians*, Homily 1:1.
4. Lightfoot, *St. Paul's Epistles to the Colossians and to Philemon*, 131.
5. Calvin, *Philippians, Colossians, and Thessalonians*, 137.
6. MacDonald, *Colossians, Ephesians*, 33–35.

this reason the community is urgently warned and admonished concerning the distinction between correct and false preaching: 'Be on your guard that no one snares you by philosophy and empty deceit' (2:8)."[7] For the most part Paul encourages them to continue in their faith, with this single proviso.[8] Wright comments, "Paul does not come before the Colossians simply as a private individual, but as an apostle of Christ Jesus."[9]

Paul associates himself with Timothy (v. 1) because his ministry is always exercised in collaboration with his many fellow workers. He is not a lone apostle or a lone missionary pastor. Timothy is named as co-worker with Paul in five other epistles: 1 and 2 Thessalonians, 2 Corinthians, Philippians., and Philemon. Timothy was converted on Paul's first missionary journey at Lystra. Elsewhere Silas, Tertius, and Sosthenes are mentioned as co-workers. Some also served as Paul's secretaries.[10] Paul was never ministering alone but always associated himself with a fellow worker or workers. E. F. Scott suggests that early Christian missionaries often worked in pairs, "perhaps in accordance with Jesus' own injunction when he sent out the disciples by two and two (Mark 6:7)."[11] Thus, O'Brien observes, "There is no suggestion of high-handedness on Paul's part when he styles himself an 'apostle.'"[12]

It need not surprise us that Paul does not use the word "church" in the address and greeting. The word is omitted in Romans, Philippians, and Ephesians, and in any case he uses the synonym "saints" or "holy ones" (Gk, *hagiois*), which denotes all Christians. Paul usually praises his readers (faithful and holy ones) before addressing any deficiency. If, as is likely, the Colossian

---

7. Lohse, *Colossians and Philemon*, 2.

8. Hooker, "Were There False Teachers in Colossae?" possibly marks the beginnings of a general turning point.

9. Wright, *Colossians and Philemon*, 49 (his italics).

10. See Richards, *Paul and First-Century Letter Writing*, especially 81–93; and Richards, *The Secretary in the Letters of Paul*.

11. Scott, *The Epistles to the Colossians, to Philemon, and to the Ephesians*, 13.

12. O'Brien, *Colossians, Philemon*, 2.

church was mainly gentile, the application of this term is remarkable, as formerly characterizing only the people of Israel. In the very earliest years, Scott observes, the term "Christians" was still a somewhat contemptuous one. Hence, Paul uses the term "saints" to lift them to higher things.[13]

The use of grace (Gk, *charis*) and peace (Gk, *eirēnē*, Heb, *shalom*) only partly reflects conventional forms of greeting. Paul speaks of "grace" with the Christian content of God's undeserved favor, especially in forgiveness and reconciliation, while "peace" does not primarily denote inner tranquility but a relation of harmony with God and well-being in general. The wish for God to be gracious and to give his peace comes in the priestly blessing of Num 6:24–26, and as Father God is the source of all blessings.

Questions for reflection

1. Why does Paul associate Timothy with him? Is there more than one reason for this? What lessons can be learned for us from Paul's being collaborative?

2. Who are "the holy people" or "the saints"? What is their relation to the people of Israel?

3. How does calling other Christians "holy" or "saints" help us not to disparage fellow-Christians?

4. Why does Paul allude to the will of God in a greeting? Can Christians appoint themselves to a ministry?

2. Reasons for Paul's thankfulness (1:3–8)

3 We always give thanks for you to God the Father of our Lord Jesus Christ in our prayers, 4 because we have heard of your faith in Christ Jesus and of the love that you show for all the saints. 5 We give thanks also because

13. Scott, *Colossians, Philemon, and Ephesians*, 14.

of the hope that has been laid up for you in heaven. You heard of this beforehand in the word of truth, the gospel that has come to you, **6** just as it is bearing fruit and increasing in the whole world, even as it makes its presence felt among you, from the day on which you heard and came to know the grace of God for what it truly is.**7** You learned this from beloved Epaphras, our fellow servant, who is a faithful minister of Christ on our behalf, **8** who declared to us your love in the Spirit.[14]

In 1:3–5, Paul begins his prayer with thanksgiving. The plural "we give thanks" is probably a literary plural, but Paul often varies between the singular and plural.[15] Lincoln comments that this "so-called intercessory prayer report" is not addressed to God but to the readers.[16] He adds that this verse does not give warrant for using public prayer "to preach or to direct subtle messages to the congregation."[17] The emphasis on God may be to affirm his sovereignty. The reasons for his thankfullness are based on six facts: first, his report of the church from Epaphras; second, the news of its faith, hope, and love, and indeed love for all the saints, or all Christians; third, the hope that is "laid up" for the church in heaven; fourth, the vibrant, increasing, response to the gospel that is evident not only at Colossae, but everywhere; fifth, the collaborative work of Epaphras as a faithful fellow-minister; and sixth, their participation in the Holy Spirit, demonstrated in their love. Prayer here and in early Christian tradition more broadly was *to* God the Father *through* the Lord Jesus Christ. Scott points out that

14. Textual notes: In v. 3 "to God the Father" is supported by B (Vaticanus), the corrector of C (C*) and Augustine. The UBS Committee "narrowly" supports it in view of other textual readings (Metzger, *A Textual Commentary on the Greek New Testament*, 552). In v. 7 the very early manuscript Ᵽ46, the corrector of Sinaiticus (ℵ), A, B, C, and D* (the Western text) read "on our behalf," which Dunn, Martin, Moule, NJB, and NIV follow (Dunn, *Colossians and Philemon*, 65; Martin, *Colossians and Philemon*, 49; Moule, *Epistles to the Colossians and to Philemon*, 27 and 51). On the other hand some MSS read "on your behalf," which is followed by the NRSV.

15. Cf. Schubert, *Form and Function of Pauline Thanksgivings*.

16. Lincoln, *Letter to the Colossians*, 590.

17. Lincoln, *Letter to the Colossians*, 594.

on this basis Christians may approach God with the confidence and trust that Jesus showed.[18]

Paul has already grouped together the triad, faith, hope, and love, in 1 Cor 13:13. This grouping is already found in other New Testament writings, especially Pauline, either explicitly or by implication (Rom 5:1–5; Gal 5:5–6; 1 Thess 1:3; Heb 6:10–12). The use of "laid up" (Gk, *apokeimeinēn*) underlines the objective and given nature of hope. The word is derived from the Greek *apothēsaurizō*, to store away for the future (1 Tim 6:19). It also occurs in Matt 6:20 (of treasure in heaven) and Luke 19:20 (of the pound wrapped up or set aside in a cloth). "Hope that is laid up" is the source of the Colossians' faith and love, and of Paul's thanksgiving.[19] NJB reads "stored up." Dunn observes, "The gospel is summed up here in terms of 'hope.'"[20] As Moule comments, "'Hope' in this distinctively Christian sense is anything but . . . a mere prize 'in the sky' reserved only for the future" because "it is a potent incentive to action here and now."[21] Hope is for the future, and the future is still hidden, but the future is absolutely secure. Lincoln observes that evidence of the readers' love is seen in their concern for other people's lives.[22]

In 1:6–8, Paul's reference to "the whole world" or to "all the world" (NJB, "throughout the world") expresses not only the dynamic growth of the gospel, but also its universality. Lincoln calls it "prophetic optimism."[23] "You heard beforehand" translates a single Greek verb (*proakouō*). Many commentators assume that "before" alludes to a time before they faced the error or "philosophy" that confronts the church. This view was proposed by J. B. Lightfoot and is adopted by Moule, i.e., they had heard the truth of the gospel before they were exposed to the falsehood that invaded the church. Danker, however, translates the verb "to hear (something)

18. Scott, *Colossians, Philemon and Ephesians*, 15.

19. Caird, *Paul's Letters from Prison*, 167.

20. Dunn, *Colossians and Philemon*, 60.

21. Moule, *The Epistles to the Colossians and to Philemon*, 49–50.

22. Lincoln, *Colossians*, 590.

23. Lincoln, *Colossians*, 591.

beforehand" as a general reference, without a specific time, and Dunn takes the same view.[24] The Colossians had mistaken speculations for a deeper wisdom. Calvin comments, "Paul confirms the doctrine of Epaphras by giving it his approbation."[25]

The part of the verb, "to bear fruit" (Gk, *karpophoroumenon*, technically it is the present middle form) occurs elsewhere only in an inscription; (the "middle" voice is used where the subject is intimately affected by its own action).[26] The verb, however, occurs in Matt 13:23; Mark 4:20; Luke 8:15; and Rom.7:4.[27] The present tense may emphasize the continuity of the growth. Chrysostom interprets this fruit-bearing as a crop of good deeds.[28]

The Colossian Christians "heard and came to know the grace of God." The Greek *epegnōte* (to know, to look upon) is aorist, indicating point in time (technically an ingressive aorist, which denotes entering upon a past state or the beginning of a past act). With the prefix *epi,* the verb strictly means to know fully, or perhaps to comprehend. Some contrast this with the vagaries of the false "philosophy" that the Colossians face. The ministry of Epaphras was the probable source of their knowledge of Christ. The best MSS read "on our behalf," i.e., he was a fellow-servant (strictly fellow-slave) with Paul.

NJB translates: "a trustworthy deputy for us." This reflects the recent work of John Collins on the Greek word *diakonos*, used here of Epaphras in v. 7.[29] *Diakonos* also occurs in 2 Cor 6:4, 1 Thess 3:2, and elsewhere in Paul. In Christian tradition, the diaconate has been thought to represent a third order among bishops, priests/presbyters, and deacons; or a second order of presbyters and deacons. But Collins translates *diakonos* as "one who serves as an intermediary, an agent, or assistant." In the New Testament, he argues, a *diakonos* serves as a deputy or assistant to a bishop or

---

24. Danker, BDAG, 65; Dunn, *Colossians and Philemon*, 60.

25. Calvin, *Philippians, Colossians and Thessalonians*, 141.

26. Harris, *Colossians and Philemon*, 303.

27. Danker, BDAG, 510; Moule, *Colossians and Philemon*, 50.

28. Chrysostom, *Homilies on Colossians*, Hom. 1, 259.

29. Collins, *Diakonia*.

presbyter. The deacon need not be equivalent to a social worker or financial administrator. Danker follows Collins, although he recognizes that Acts 6:2 (serving at tables) constitutes a "special problem."[30]

Epaphras told Paul of their love in (the) Spirit. Moule comments that the absence of the definite article does not imply that Paul does not intend this to mean the Holy Spirit.[31] Otherwise, he hardly mentions the Holy Spirit in this epistle.

Questions for reflection

1. What place do we give to thanksgiving in our prayers?
2. For what does Paul especially thank God?
3. What is the force of saying that hope is "laid up" in heaven?
4. Do we sometimes set faith and love in contrast to each other when they are complementary?
5. Why is Paul so grateful that the gospel has reached "the whole world"?
6. Paul calls the gospel the word of truth. Is truth becoming sacrificed to pleasure?

3. Intercession through Christ, who rescues us from darkness (1:9–14)

9 That is why, from the first day that we heard it, we do not cease to give thanks for you, praying and asking that you may be filled with full knowledge of his will in spiritual wisdom and understanding, 10 that you may walk worthily of the Lord with a view to being pleasing to him in all respects, bearing fruit in every good work, and growing in the full knowledge of God. 11 Being

30. Danker, BDAG, 229–31; cf. Croft, *Ministry in Three Dimensions*.
31. Moule, *Colossians and Philemon*, 52.

strengthened with all power according to the strength
of his glory, with a view to perseverance and endurance
with joy. **12** We give thanks to the Father, who has made
us sufficient to share the lot of the inheritance of God's
holy people in light. **13** God has rescued you from the
power of darkness and transferred us into the kingdom
of his beloved Son, **14** in whom we have redemption, the
forgiveness of our sins.[32]

Lohse points out that vv. 9–11 repeat much of what Paul has already said in vv. 4–6.[33] Yet a comparison with Eph 1:8–14 shows that Paul (or the Pauline author of Ephesians) prays with repetitions without hesitation. Murray Harris observes, "This refers to prayer that is regular and frequent rather than uninterrupted."[34]

"The knowledge of his will" (Gk, *tēn epignōsin tou thelēmatos*) uses a Hellenistic or Koine word for full knowledge. The word occurs in Polybius and Plutarch, for example. Some suggest that this anticipates the "gnostic" error of claims to a "private" or secret revelation.[35] Paul refers to practical knowledge of God, not to speculative, human-made knowledge. The cure for intellectual upstarts is not ignorance nor obscurantism, but knowledge of the will of God. Today we have overreacted against intellectual knowledge. "Spiritual" (Gk, *pneumatikē*) probably qualifies both wisdom and understanding, as the translation implies. "Spiritual" refers to the Holy Spirit's work of illumination. This is not a merely

---

32. Textual notes: v. 12 "presents a curious nest of variant readings" (Metzger, *Textual Commentary*, 553). First, "to the Father" is supported by various witnesses including Þ61, C*, F, and G. Second, the phrase "made us sufficient" (Gk, *hikanōsanti*) or "made us able" (NJB) is supported by Þ46, Sinaiticus, A, C, and Dc. But several Western texts (D*, F, G and 33) substitute "called" (Gk, *kalesaanti)*. This arose either accidentally or in transcription as a substitution for a rare and unexpected word. "Made us sufficient" (Gk, *hikanōsanti*) occurs in the New Testament only in 2 Cor 3:6. Third, in this verse, Sinaiticus and B read "you" (Gk, *humas*), while A, C, and D read "us" (Gk, *hēmas*). A majority of the UBS Committee preferred the "you" reading.

33. Lohse, *Colossians and Philemon*, 25.

34. Harris, *Colossians and Philemon*, 29.

35. Bruce with Simpson, *Epistles of Paul to the Ephesians and to the Colossians*.

intellectual knowledge. Lohse and O'Brien describe these verses as a sort of introit that introduces the solemn christological hymn in vv. 15–20.[36] O'Brien rightly suggests that "deliver" (Gk, *rhuesthai*), "transfer" (Gk, *methistanai*), "light" (Gk, *phōs*), "share" (Gk, *meris*), and "lot" (Gk, *klēros*) may well imply a baptismal context. This may partly answer Dunn's concern that these are not usual Pauline words.

In 1:10, Paul says that right knowledge will enable the Colossians to live in a manner worthy of the holiness of God who has called them. "Wisdom" was probably a catchword of many Asian communities.[37] Lincoln notes that for all its use of the term "philosophy" the false teaching has only the appearance of wisdom.[38] As Bruce comments on v. 11, "Paul prays that they may be endowed not only with knowledge but with power."[39] Paul repeats his assurance in 2 Cor 3:6 that God is their sufficiency. The readers' power, Lincoln suggests, enables them to please God, and to face trials, distractions, and opposition.[40] In v. 13, Paul continues this baptismal or conversion terminology. God has rescued them (Gk, *errysato*) from the power of darkness. He has used a different word, but a parallel thought in Gal 1:4, when he says that God has delivered or rescued them (Gk, *exeletai*, technically, aorist middle subjunctive of *exaireō*, to deliver or to rescue) "out of this present evil world" (the "middle" voice, we noted, represents the subject as intimately affected by its own action).

In vv. 11–13, Paul uses almost a tautology, "empowered with all power," or "strengthened with all power according to the strength of his glory," by using the Greek word *dynamoumenoi* (present passive of *dynamoō*), with *kata to kratos tēs doxēs autou* (according to the strength of his glory) where *kratos* also denotes strength. "To share" or "to have a share in" (Gk, *eis merida*), where Greek *meros*, a share or a portion, means a share of their

---

36. Lohse, *Colossians and Philemon*; O'Brien, *Colossians, Philemon*, 25.

37. Deissmann, *Bible Studies*, 42–48.

38. Lincoln, *Colossians*, 592.

39. Bruce with Simpson, *Ephesians and Colossians*, 187.

40. Lincoln, *Colossians*, 593.

inheritance (Gk, *klērou*). *Kleros* in origin denoted a pebble or piece or wood used in casting lots (Acts 8:21), and then came to denote the allotted portion or inheritance, as in v. 12.[41] Paul wants to express to his mainly gentile Christians the immense privileges that they have received as God's reconstituted Israel. Wesley observes, "Suffer it to the end, not barely with patience, but with thankful joy."[42] "Perseverance" is a better and stronger word than "patience," as Synge observes.[43] Their wavering strength should not discourage them because God is at work. Paul calls not for a dull Stoical endurance, but for a cheerful confidence. Calvin comments, however, "Paul puts them in mind of their own weakness, for he says that they will not be strong otherwise than by the Lord's help . . . according to his glorious power."[44]

The words "redemption" and "redeem" in v. 14 have deep roots in the Old Testament (Heb., *pādāh*, to redeem or ransom, *peduth*, redemption; *gā'al*, to redeem; Gk *apolutrōsis*, redemption or ransom). Israel was redeemed from Egypt and from bondage, just as Christians are redeemed from the powers of darkness. Israel was redeemed by God's mighty arm, just as Christians are redeemed by God's power and the strength of his glory in Christ. Israel was redeemed to freedom and new life in the promised land, just as Christians are redeemed to forgiveness of sins and a portion of the inheritance. In both cases, redemption entails redemption *from* a condition of jeopardy, by a costly act of God, *to* a new life of forgiveness and freedom. The word would also be familiar with the practice of slavery, indicating release from bondage.

Ephesians 6:12 also speaks of principalities and powers, darkness, and wickedness. The Old Testament looks forward to God's victory over such hostile powers. The Colossian Christians are "removed from a world which is subject to evil forces."[45] Scott comments that often today we speak not of "angelic powers throned

---

41. Danker, BDAG, 548.

42. Wesley, *Colossians*, 10.

43. F Synge, *Philippians and Colossians*, 65.

44. Calvin, *Philippians, Colossians, and Thessalonians*, 144.

45. Scott, *Colossians, Philemon, and Ephesians*, 18

in the planets, but of a world of mechanical law, in the clutches of which we are helpless . . . [, but] we have access to a world of freedom. God has delivered us out of the lower mechanical sphere and placed us in the kingdom of his Son."[46]

Questions for reflection

1. How does wisdom differ from knowledge? Where is wisdom expounded?

2. What are lives worthy of the Lord?

3. What contexts are suggested by "rescue," "transfer," "endure," and "light"?

4. Which three aspects of "redemption" most readily spring to mind?

5. What role is implied for the work of the Holy Spirit?

46. *Scott, Colossians, Philemon, and Ephesians*, 19.

II

Doctrine

The Universal Lordship and All-Sufficiency of Christ

1:15—2:23

1. The supremacy and sufficiency of Jesus Christ (1:15–23)

15 He [Christ] is the image of the unseen God, the first-born of all creation, **16** because in him all things were created, both in heaven and on the earth, things visible and invisible, whether thrones or dominions or principalities or powers; all things were created through him, and for him. **17** He himself exists before all things, and in him all things achieve a coherent focus. **18** He is the Head of his Body, the church. He is the beginning, the first-born from the dead, in order that he might come to have the first place in every way. **19** For in him all the fullness of God was pleased to dwell, **20** and through him to reconcile all things to himself, having made peace through the blood of his cross, whether things on earth, or things in heaven. 21 Once you were in a state of alienation and hostile in your minds, doing evil deeds 22 but he now reconciled you in his fleshly body to present you holy and blameless and irreproachable before him 23 —as long as you continue firmly established and steadfast in faith and never letting yourselves be moved from the hope of the gospel that you heard, which has been preached to every created being under heaven, and of which I, Paul, have become a servant.[1]

Lincoln writes, "Christ is the one who supremely makes the invisible God visible."[2] Many say that vv. 15–20 offer the highest conception of the person of Christ in all the Pauline writings, comparable with that of John. Other writers consider that these verses are a pre-Pauline hymn or creed on the supremacy and all-sufficiency of Christ in creation and redemption. The reasons for this latter hypothesis are mainly stylistic and based on the unusual vocabulary. The NJB prints vv. 15–20 as poetry, although the NRSV and NIV print it as prose.

James Robinson argues strongly for the poetic form of vv. 15–20.[3] Ernst Käsemann long ago in 1949 had argued for the hymnic character of these verses, as well as the influence of Luke.[4] Many commentators are convinced that the poetic creed is a shared pre-Pauline formulation. F. F. Bruce and A. M. Hunter are among these writers, citing also 1 Cor 8:1–4 in this regard.[5] They quote the

1. Textual note. The manuscript readings of v. 22 are "difficult to resolve" according to the UBS Committee (Metzger, *A Textual Commentary*, 554–55). The Greek *apokatēllaxen* (he has reconciled) is well supported by Ᵽ46, Sinaiticus, A, C, and D, but it is difficult to explain why other readings (e.g., B) arose (B has the imperative "be reconciled"), and the passive voice seems odd. Lightfoot followed B (Vaticanus). A majority of the Committee, however, favored retaining the reading, but with "a high degree of doubt."

2. Lincoln, *Colossians*, 597.

3. Robinson, "A Formal Analysis of Colossians 1:15–20"; cf. also Hammerton-Kelly, *Pre-existence, Wisdom, and the Son of Man*, 168–74.

4. Käsemann, "A Primitive Christian Baptismal Liturgy."

5. Bruce, *Colossians*, 192–94; Hunter, *Paul and His Predecessors*.

Old Testament passages that influenced them (e.g., Prov 8:22–31), together with parallels in Heb 1:2–4 and John 1:1–4.

Scot McKnight, however, is more cautious, especially in view of the work of Matthew Gordley.[6] Gordley cites four clear divergences from the classic form of ancient hymnody: lack of consistent meter, a lack of invocation, a lack of petition or request, and current location in the letter.[7] McKnight does cite some counterbalancing arguments, including the tendency of early Christians to use corporate song. He notes, "The earliest Christians sang with one another (1 Cor. 14:26; Col. 3:16; Eph. 5:19–20; Rev. 4:11; 5:9–10; 15:3–4; 19)."[8] That does not, of course, mean that Col 1:15–20 contains one of those songs. McKnight thus leaves open the issue of whether Paul used, but modified, earlier Christian material.

It seems strange that while many have argued for an earlier, *pre*-Pauline date, many others regard the Christology, which suggests the incarnation and even the deity of Christ, to be pointing to a *post*-Pauline development. Obviously the material cannot be both pre- and post-Pauline! Ralph Martin examines the parallel passage of Phil 2:5–11 and argues that a high Christology should not be taken as an indication of a late text. There is a growing trend among New Testament scholars to defending the existence of high Christology from very early in the post-Jesus period.[9] Many support the existence of high Christology from very early in the post-Jesus period.[10] Thus, the theology provides no strong reason to see the material as post-Pauline and certainty eludes us in claiming its origins as pre-Pauline, though it is certainly possible.

The image of the unseen God (v. 15) is that which makes God visible and concrete. He who sees Jesus has seen God (John 14:9). John 1:18 asserts that no one has ever seen God, but the Son has

6. McKnight, *Letter to the Colossians*, 132–38.

7. Gordley, *The Colossian Hymn in Context*; and Gordley, *Teaching through Song in Antiquity*.

8. McKnight, *Letter to the Colossians*, 135.

9. Hurtado, *Lord Jesus Christ*; Hurtado, *One God, One Lord*; Bauckham, *God Crucified*; and Fletcher-Louis, *Jesus Monotheism*.

10. Martin, *Carmen Christi*.

made him known. Romans 1:20 also declares that God is unseen but may be perceived through his creation. In 2 Cor 4:4–6 God caused the light of the gospel of the glory of God to shine in the face of Jesus Christ. Hebrews 1:3 similarly describes Christ as "the radiance of God's glory" and the exact essence of God's very being. "First-born" (Gk, *prōtotokos*), here, means having first place in cosmic terms, as suggested by the five passages just quoted that speak of Christ as having the highest place over all creation. That "firstborn" means "first in status" rather than "first created" is also suggested by 1:16, which reads *"For* by him all things were created." The "for" in 1:16 suggests that what follows is offered in support of the firstborn claim in 1:15. However, if firstborn literally means first created it seems odd to support that claim with an argument that all created things were created through him (for he would be one of the "all" things that were created). However, if "firstborn" means "first in status" then such a claim *would* be supported by the assertion that all created things were created through him.

High, incarnational Christology is not peculiar to Colossians. Moulton and Milligan and Deissmann also find this word "first-born" in inscriptions and in the papyri.[11] It cannot be used as Arius used it, to imply that Christ is a creature alongside all creation. The emphasis is on the comparative or superlative force of "first" (Gk, *prōtos*). In contrast to the "gnostic" false "philosophy" Christ is the exact image of God, the location of true knowledge of God. "First-born" also echoes the words of Ps 89:27, spoken of the Davidic king. Christ is before all creation.

Some suggest that these verses reflect an Alexandrian concept of the Logos as the Word which existed from the beginning within the being of God, and through whom God created the universe. But parallels do not prove cause or origin. Paul may have been in contact with Alexandrian ideas through his fellow worker Apollos or simply through ides that were in the air. 1 Corinthians 8:6 shows how early Paul formulated such ideas of God. He would certainly have developed his thinking in the face of the false

---

11. Moulton and Milligan, *Vocabulary of the New Testament*, 557; Deissmann, *Light from the Ancient East*, 88.

teachers in Colossae. Christ is significant not only for salvation, but in relation to the cosmos.

In 2 Cor 4:4 Paul has already described Christ as the image or likeness of God. Similarly, in 1 Cor 11:7 Christ is "the image and glory of God." The "image of God" concept reflects Gen 1:26–27, where God created humanity in his own image to display to the rest of creation the character of God. In the ancient world, pagan temples would regularly present images of their deities to display something about these deities. Israel was forbidden to make carved images of God as mere objects, because being the image of God was Israel's own special vocation (though Israel failed to display the character of God adequately). Yet Christ in Col 1:15–20 is also *prior* to creation, not a mere created image as Adam or Israel were. The true image of God was seen only in Christ.

The Russian Orthodox theologian Vladimir Lossky carefully argues that to show forth God's image is not a natural capacity of people but is acquired only by grace through being restored in Christ.[12] What are we to make of Lossky's approach? We might well agree with Douglas Moo's statement, "In Col. 3:10 . . . Paul says that the 'the new self' is 'being renewed in knowledge in the image of its Creator.'"[13] In Col 3:10, the new believer is renewed in the image of God as the goal.

"In 1 Cor. 15:49 and 2 Cor. 4:4," writes Lincoln, "Paul had used the term 'image' (*eikōn*) for the resurrected and exalted Christ, who as the last Adam now represents humanity as God had always intended it to be."[14] Lincoln also points out that "Firstborn" shows that Christ is "the first of God's acts," while Wisdom is spoken of in Proverbs as the beginning of God's work, and even as "firstborn" in Philo.[15] Burney, Davies, Caird, Wright, and Lincoln emphasize the influence of the Old Testament on this hymn.[16] Calvin points

12. Lossky, *In the Image and Likeness of God*, 155; and Lossky, *The Mystical Theology of the Eastern Church*, 117.

13. Moo, *Letters to Colossians and to Philemon*, 117.

14. Lincoln, *Colossians*, 597.

15. Lincoln, *Colossians*, 597.

16. Burney, "Christ as the Archē of Creation"; Davies, *Paul and Rabbinic*

out that "First born" establishes not only Christ's priority in time (i.e., before all creation), but the term is also used "because he was begotten by the Father, that they might be created by him, and that he might be, as it were, the substance or foundation of all things."[17]

In v. 16, "All things" were created (Gk, *ektisthē*) in him, as John 1:3 and Heb 1:2 also state. This verse expounds what being "the first-born of creation" entails. "All things" was a well-known philosophical phrase for "the universe," which Paul uses in Rom 11:35-36. McKnight comments, "A noticeable theme . . . is the word 'all' (1:15; 16 [bis], 17 [bis] 18, 19, 20, a term that captures not only the cosmic and universal scope of the Son's embodied lordship and redemption . . . but also the substantial concern the apostle has in his mission with reconciling Jews and Gentiles, slaves and freed, males and females."[18] The whole of God's creative activity is summed up in Christ, including the creation of heavenly beings, such as angels, and earthly beings, whether dignitaries or ordinary people. Through Christ all things have their unity and meaning. There are four classes of heavenly beings that Paul mentions: "thrones" (Gk, *thronoi*), "dominions" (Gk, *kyriotētes*), "principalities" (Gk, *archai*), and "powers" (Gk, *exousiai*). What precisely are these different kinds of beings?

Marianne Meye Thompson includes an excursus on "Principalities and Powers." She writes, "Unfortunately Paul never goes into detail about the precise identity of any of these groups, for he seems to assume that the readers will understand the sorts of figures to which he is referring. . . . The principalities and powers are real. . . . They meet us as embodied in visible and tangible realities—people, nations, and institutions. And they are powerful."[19]

In v. 16, Paul uses *ktizō* (to create) in both the aorist (*ektisthē*), for a definite creative act of God in the past, and the perfect

---

Judaism, 150-52; Caird, *Letters from Prison*, 175; Wright, "Poetry and Theology in Colossians 1:15-20"; Lincoln, *Colossians*, 604.

17. Calvin, *Philippians, Colossians, and Thessalonians*, 150.

18. McKnight, *Letter to the Colossians*, 137.

19. Thompson, *Colossians and Philemon*, 34; cf. 36-39.

(*ektistai*), meaning "remain created" as his creatures. Thus, both the *origin* and *permanence* of creation rests in Christ.

Christ, for Paul, is the intermediate sustaining agent of creation: the universe is *through* (Gk, *dia*) him, but it is also *"to him"* (Gk, *kai eis auton*), and in him all things "hold together" (v. 17). In other words, Christ is the agent through whom and for whom God created everything, creation's origin and destiny. And he is the agent through whom God sustains it in being.

Sylvia Keesmaat argues, "The challenge that Colossians provides to its imperial context is overwhelmingly rooted in a strong theology of creation. Paul describes himself as the servant of a gospel that has 'been proclaimed to every creature under heaven' (1:23)."[20] This comes after the hymn of 1:15–20 in which Paul asserts that all things in heaven and on earth were created in Christ, through Christ, and for Christ.

In vv. 19–20, Paul also brings together "in him," "through him," and "to him" in the context of incarnation and redemption. This is not entirely novel, except that elsewhere "from" applies only to God: Rom 11:36 is otherwise similar, "From him and through him and to him are all things. To him be glory for ever." Christ is mediate creator (the universe is created *through* him); God is its ultimate source (the universe is *from* him). A. T. Robertson points out that we have the same distinction in 1 Cor 8:6, "the Father, *from whom* all things . . . exist" and "Jesus Christ *through whom* are all things." In this respect, creation and redemption are parallel: both are *from* God and *through* Christ. Christ is thus Mediator in both creation and redemption. Martin writes, "No [other] Jewish thinker ever rose to these heights in daring to predict that Wisdom was the ultimate goal of all creation."[21]

It is a matter of historical and linguistic interest that Stoic philosophers used similar language. The Emperor Marcus Aurelius wrote, "O Nature . . . all things come from you, subsist in you, go back to you."[22] But, as O'Brien and Bruce point out, linguistic

20. Keesmaat, "Colossians," 122.

21. Martin, *Colossians*, 58.

22. Marcus Aurelius, *Meditations*, 4.23; O'Brien, *Colossians*, 45; Lohse,

affinities do not necessarily imply identity of meaning. There are plenty of Old Testament precedents, including Genesis 1, Proverbs 8, and other texts in Jewish Wisdom literature that suggest Paul's vocabulary. Scott comments, "It is the same thought which the writer of Revelation expresses when he calls Christ the Alpha and Omega."[23] McKnight comments, "The Jewish wisdom tradition does not explain all of the Christology in this hymn, but it sets up a context for us to ponder the magnitude of apostolic hermeneutics that seek to comprehend the meaning of Jesus in God's plan for history."[24]

Lohse interprets the Greek *synestēken* in v. 17 (perfect tense) to mean "are established," in contrast to the mixture of tenses in v. 16 (i.e., "in him all things are established").[25] But the verb means "to be in a coherent state." In Ben Sirach 43:26 and in Philo (*Quis rerum divinarum heres*, 23.188) it means "hold together," a meaning adopted by the NJB. Hellenistic synagogues also used such language of creation. Lohse offers the phrase "the unifying bond."[26] Danker lists "to bring into existence in an organized manner," "to put together," "to be in a condition of coherence."[27] Dunn renders it "hold the universe together."[28] We suggest "achieves a coherent focus." Harris rightly comments, "What Christ has created he maintains in permanent order, stability, and productivity. He is the source of the unity . . . and cohesiveness . . . of the whole universe."[29]

In "He is the head of the body" (v. 18), "head" (Gk, *kephalē*) is used not primarily in a physiological sense, but in the sense of "ruler," and Christ is head not only of the church, but also of the

Colossians and Philemon, 49; Norden, *Agnostos Theos*.

23. Scott, *Colossians, Philemon, and Ephesians*, 22

24. McKnight, *Letter to the Colossians*, 143. Cf. Bauckham "Where is Wisdom to be Found? (Colossians 1:15–20."

25. Lohse, *Colossians and Philemon*, 49.

26. Lohse, *Colossians and Philemon*, 52.

27. Danker, BDAG, 973.

28. Dunn, *Colossians and Philemon*, 94.

29. Harris, *Colossians and Philemon*, 47.

cosmos.[30] The Hebrew *r'sh* (head) is also capable of meaning either physiological head or especially chief or topmost.[31] The purpose clause is "that in all things he might come to have the first place" (Gk, *hina genētai en pasin autos prōteuōn*). The Greek *prōteuōn* means to hold the highest rank in a group, or to have first place.[32] Lohse provides numerous historical and linguistic parallels from Hellenistic sources including Plato, the Stoics, and Philo.[33] But Paul has already elaborated the image of the body of Christ for the church in 1 Cor 12:12–27 and Rom 12:4–5. Calvin comments, "Christ alone has authority to govern the Church. . . . On [Christ] alone the unity of the body depends."[34]

The image of the body was a familiar example of the common life and mutual interdependence of a political or social group. Menenius Agrippa used it to persuade rebelling workers of Rome not to act against patricians on the ground that to starve part of the body would bring disaster on the whole body.

Bruce comments that it is unlikely that Paul drew here on Stoic sources in his use of body imagery, and indeed J. A. T. Robinson suggests that it perhaps originated in his conversion experience.[35] Bruce suggests that Paul may have drawn on rabbinic speculation about Adam.[36] At all events, he concludes, "When we speak of the Church as the body of Christ, we think of it as being vitalized by his presence with it and his risen life in it."[37] Thornton compares it to the organic image of the vine in John 15.[38]

---

30. Schweizer, "*sōma*"; and Bedale, "The Meaning of *kephalē* in the Pauline Epistles."

31. Brown, Driver, Briggs, *The New BDB Hebrew and English Lexicon*, 910–11.

32. Danker, BDAG, 892.

33. Lohse, *Colossians*, 53–55.

34. Calvin, *Philippians, Colossians, and Thessalonians*, 152.

35. Bruce, *Colossians*, 203; Robinson, *The Body*, 78–79.

36. Bruce, *Colossians*, 203.

37. Bruce, *Colossians*, 204.

38. Thornton, *The Common Life in the Body of Christ*, 144.

That Christ is also "the beginning" (Gk, *hē archē*) in v. 18 implies his pre-existence. Furthermore, Christ is not only the "first-born of all creation" (v. 15) but also the "first-born from the dead" (v. 18)—note the parallel. That is to say, Christ is the first-born of the *new* creation, which is what his resurrection inaugurates and instantiates. Calvin comments, "In the resurrection there is a restoration of all things."[39] Christ is supreme then both in this creation (which was made through and for him) and in the new creation (which his resurrection brings to birth).

In fact, it is arguably the resurrection itself which inspired the subsequent perception of Christ's role in the original divine act of creation. We may note Lincoln's view, "Without a belief that God raised Jesus from the dead or some experience of Christ's aliveness, there is little incentive to think of Jesus as any more than a Jewish prophet, sage, social revolutionary, or healer."[40] But in light cast by the resurrection, Christ's cosmic significance was illuminated in fresh and profound ways.

The Greek of v. 19 does not explicitly include the word "God." But Lohse rightly comments, "The Greek text permits that 'God' could be supplied as subject . . . 'God was pleased to let all the fullness dwell in him.' This would achieve a smooth connection to the following participle 'He (God) was making peace.'"[41] He adds, "The words 'all the fullness' mean nothing else than the divine fullness in its totality . . . the whole fullness of deity."[42] N. T. Wright agrees.[43]

The word "fullness" was almost certainly used by those to whom Paul referred when he warned the Christians in Colossae not to be corrupted by false teachers and their "philosophy." If these were "gnostics," "fullness" may have denoted (for them) emanations between God and the world. These were allegedly intermediaries, whereas Paul insists that *Christ alone* mediates between

39. Calvin. *Philippians, Colossians, and Thessalonians*, 153.
40. Lincoln, Colossians, 607.
41. Lohse, *Colossians*, 56.
42. Lohse, *Colossians*, 57.
43. Wright, *Colossians and Philemon*, 80.

God and the world. Harris points out that "fullness" can either be understood impersonally (as Lohse and Hübner do) or personally to denote "God in all his fullness" (as Moule, Wright, and O'Brien do).[44] Harris argues for the latter.[45] Dunn comments further, "The idea of God or his Spirit as filling the world is another way of expressing the divine rationality that permeates the world in Stoic thought."[46] Nevertheless, Dunn insists on the Hebrew origin of this idea in the Wisdom literature alongside resonances with Stoicism. Lincoln acknowledges that while for Paul we have an overarching narrative of Christ from creation to the consummation, today many postmodernists regard "grand narratives" with suspicion.[47] He therefore bids us remember the poetic form of this hymn about Christ. On the other hand, we may also question in what sense postmodernists such as J-F Lyotard critique the role of "grand narratives." Arguably metanarratives of the kind Scripture offers do not fall foul of their objections.

It was God's decree and good pleasure, Paul continues in v. 20, to reconcile (Gk, *katallassō*) all things to himself. It was part of Paul's genius to introduce the word "reconciliation" with God to denote the reversal of sinners' situation of alienation from God, or even hostility toward him. The Greek noun denotes the re-establishment of an interrupted or broken relationship, while the verb denotes "the exchange of hostility for a friendly relationship."[48] Whereas many theological terms require a knowledge of Old Testament uses, this term remains utterly familiar in the secular world, both then and now. Here Paul uses the verb with a double compound (*apo* + *kata*), *apokatallaxai,* which occurs only here. Robertson suggests that the double compound indicates complete reconciliation.[49]

---

44. Hübner, "*Plērōma*"; Moule, *Colossians and Philemon,* 70–71.

45. Harris, *Colossians and Philemon,* 49; Wright, *Colossians and Philemon,* 79.

46. Dunn, *Colossians and Philemon,* 99.

47. Lincoln, *Colossians,* 609.

48. Danker, BDAG, 521.

49. A. T. Robertson, *Word Pictures in the New Testament,* vol. 4, 481.

The word refers to relations of estrangement or harmony between husband and wife, parents and children, nations or states at war or in peace, industrial relations between employers and employees, and many other areas of everyday life. One classic verse from Paul on this theme is Rom 5:12: "If while we were enemies, we were reconciled to God through the death of his Son, much more surely, having been reconciled, will we be saved by his life." (In Rom 5:1, Paul speaks of "peace with God," which is another way of expressing reconciliation with God.) Paul also uses the words in Rom 5:10–11; 11:15; and 1 Cor 7:11 (of husband and wife). In 2 Cor 5:18–19 reconciliation is fully transparent in meaning, where Paul speaks of his gospel ministry as "the ministry of reconciliation." The message in 2 Cor 5:20, "Be reconciled to God," is clear. Here in Colossians, outside the four major epistles, Paul states, "God was pleased to reconcile to himself all things."

In the early twentieth century, James Denney insisted that reconciliation "is a work which is finished . . . a work outside of us, in which God so deals in Christ with the sin of the world that it shall no longer be a barrier between himself and man."[50] Denney is surely right to emphasize the finished nature of reconciliation in terms of the atonement, even though through the Holy Spirit it is also to be appropriated in life. Hence, having told us that "God was in Christ reconciling the world to himself" (2 Cor 5:19), a completed work, Paul urges, "We beseech you on behalf of Christ, *be reconciled* to God" (2 Cor 5:20).

In Col 1:20 the language about the reconciliation of all things raises the question of whether reconciliation with God is universal, i.e., for all people. Paul's language does indeed embrace the cosmos with its language about all things on earth and things in heaven. Wesley thought that "things in heaven" meant "Those who are now in paradise; the saints who died before Christ came."[51] But Paul's words appear to include fallen angels and demonic beings too. Calvin argues that "things in heaven" probably refers to

50. Denney, *The Death of Christ*, 145.
51. Wesley, *Colossians*, 14.

42

angelic beings who stand in need of reconciliation through Christ, since even angels may sin against God.[52]

So are fallen angels reconciled? Bruce comments, "It is contrary to the whole analogy of Scripture (the Pauline writings included) to apply the idea of reconciliation in the ordinary sense to fallen angels. . . . The principalities and powers whose conquest by Christ is described in 2:15 are certainly not depicted there as gladly surrendering to his grace, but as submitting against their wills to a power which they cannot resist."[53] O'Brien uses the word "pacification" to describe Bruce's approach.[54]

Bruce and O'Brien's position has merit, but is not without problems. Paul's understanding of reconciliation is clarified by adding "having made peace (Gk, *eirēnopoiēsas*) through the blood of his cross." The verb is a rare one, used only here in the New Testament, although Eph 2:15 has the word "made peace" in two separate words (Gk, *poiōn eirēnēn*). In the LXX it occurs only in Prov 10:10. Again, "peace" implies the cessation of war. References to "blood" and "his cross" underline the glory and shame of the crucifixion of Christ.[55] Dunn adds: "What is being claimed is quite simply and profoundly that the divine purpose in the act of reconciliation and peacemaking was to restore the harmony of the original creation, to bring into renewed oneness and wholeness 'all things.'"[56] That this reconciliation is a restored relationship to God is further indicated by vv. 21–22, where we read that Paul's audience are actively participating in Christ.

"Once you were in a state of alienation and hostile in your minds, doing evil deeds" (v. 21) sets in contrast the former unredeemed state of the addressees. "State of alienation" indicates being "continuously and persistently out of harmony with God, as Paul's . . . Greek puts it."[57] This is parallel with Eph 4:18. What Paul

52. Calvin, *Philippians, Colossians, and Thessalonians*, 156.

53. Bruce, *Colossians*, 210.

54. O'Brien, *Colossians*, 56.

55. Dunn, *Colossians and Philemon*, 103–4.

56. Dunn, *Colossians and Philemon*, 104.

57. Martin, *Colossians*, 66.

has described on a cosmic scale is now brought home to the addressees personally. "You" is in a prominent position in Greek. As Caird remarks, Paul's grandiose language about the cosmic Christ might seem like "castles in the air," if he did not apply the teaching personally.[58] Paul's reference to "doing evil deeds" reminds us that reconciliation with God includes changes in practical lifestyle and practical ethical goals. The phrase may refer to idolatry and immorality among gentiles (cf. Rom 1:21–32).

Verse 22 now establishes the contrary: Christians have been reconciled "in his [Christ's] fleshly body to present you holy, blameless and irreproachable before him." Christ's body of flesh (Gk, *sarx*) is a barely hidden rebuke to those false teachers who devalued the genuinely physical nature of the body of Jesus, i.e., a genuine incarnation in contrast to a "docetic" Christology. Robert Gundry has shown the importance of the physical body in Paul's thought.[59] Wesley suggests that "body of flesh" is to distinguish this from the body of the church.[60] Paul combines both Greek *sarx*, flesh, and Greek *sōma*, body.

The goal of reconciliation is to present people holy and blameless before God (v. 22). "To present" (Gk, *parastēsai*) is an infinitive of purpose. It reflects 1 Cor 1:8, and Col 2:28 repeats the thought. "Holy" (Gk, *hagious*) means "positively consecrated" (Robertson), and matches "without blemish" (Gk, *amōmous*), which is often used to denote unblemished animals set apart for sacrifice to God. "Irreproachable" (Gk, *anegklētos*) means innocent of any accusation or charge. As O'Brien observes, "The verb in the indicative is used to denote the decisive transfer of the believers from the old aeon [or old age] to the new which has taken place in the death of Christ."[61] Calvin warns us that "This holiness is nothing more than begun in us, and is indeed every day making progress, but

58. Caird, *Letters from Prison*, 182.

59. Gundry, *Sōma in Biblical Theology with Emphasis on Pauline Anthropology*, 239.

60. Wesley, *Colossians*, 14.

61. O'Brien, *Colossians*, 67.

will not be perfected until Christ shall appear for the restoration of all things."[62]

"As long as you continue . . ." in v. 23 reminds the readers that the Christian life requires constant implementation. Wesley perhaps characteristically observes, "Otherwise, ye will lose all the blessings which ye have already begun to enjoy."[63] They are to continue "firmly established [or stable] and steadfast." Martin calls these "metaphors of strength and security drawn from the picture of a house," and Lohse and Dunn agree. Lohse also cites the allusion of Jesus to "building on the rock."[64] Hence our translation, "firmly established." Paul has used this metaphor in 1 Cor 3:10–11. The point of the verse is to emphasize that Christians in Colossae must not drift away from the gospel.

As with 2 Corinthians 5, we find here a theological balance between a claim to universal reconciliation achieved in Christ (2 Cor 5:19; Col 1:20) and a clear requirement to respond aright to the gospel of peace (2 Cor 5:20; Col 1:23). So this is no universal salvation irrespective of one's response to God's reconciling work.

The gospel of which Paul is a minister has been preached to every creature under heaven (v. 23), i.e., it is universal in scope. Paul described himself and Apollos as ministers (Gk, plural, *diakonoi*, 1 Cor 3:5). We have commented earlier on the word "minister" (Gk, *diakonos*) in the light of Collins' argument that *diakonos* means one who deputizes for a bishop or presbyter (i.e., likely to belong to the "clerical" order) in contrast to the more traditional notion of financial and social ministry to the poor (largely based on Acts 6:2–4). The task of a "deacon," Collins argued, was not greatly different from that of presbyters. Both are "servants" of the gospel. Lohse calls this work "a basic function of the church."[65]

---

62. Calvin, *Philippians, Colossians, and Thessalonians*, 159.

63. Wesley, *Colossians*, 15.

64. Martin, *Colossians*, 68; Lohse, *Colossians*, 66.

65. Lohse, *Colossians and Philemon*, 67.

Questions for reflection

1. Do we lament that we cannot see the invisible God, perhaps conceiving of him as remote or distant? Does it help to see Jesus as God's gracious visible embodiment?

2. What might it mean to speak of Jesus Christ as the origin and goal of all things, including our life? How helpful is this notion?

3. How is Christ our focus of coherence, or what makes sense of everything? Can Christ "hold together" the disorganized fragments of our life in true meaning?

4. Is Christ our peacemaker with God? Which theological words in this text are easy to explain?

5. Do we adequately appreciate that without the cross of Christ we would be alienated strangers in a state of hostility with God?

6. Are we firmly established in the faith like a secure building, built on rock?

7. Are we ever tempted to add rival mediators to Jesus Christ when thinking of our relationship to God as creator and reconciler?

2. Our share in the reconciling work of God: Paul's ministry (1:24—2:5)

24 Now I rejoice in my sufferings on your behalf. In my flesh I am making up in turn what is left over of the afflictions of Christ for the sake of his body, which is the church. 25 I myself became its servant according to the responsibility given to me by God for you, to make the word of God fully completed. 26 This is the mystery that was hidden throughout the ages and generations, but has now been revealed to his holy people. 27 To them God

was pleased to make known the riches of the glory of this mystery among the gentiles, namely Christ in you, the hope of glory. **28** Him we proclaim to everyone, warning every single person and teaching every single person in all wisdom, in order to present everyone full-grown in Christ. **29** For this I labor, striving with the energy that works within me powerfully. **2:1** For I want you to know how greatly I strive for you and for those of Laodicea and as many as have not seen me face-to-face **2** in order that your hearts may be encouraged, and knit together in love so that they may have all the riches of fully assured understanding, that they may fully know the mystery of God, namely Christ. **3** In him are hidden all the treasures of wisdom and knowledge. **4** I tell you this so that no one may delude you with persuasive rhetoric. **5** For even if I am absent physically, yet I am with you in spirit, and I rejoice to see your unbroken order and the steadfastness of your faith in Christ.[66]

(a) Paul's ministry among the gentiles (1:24–25)

Regarding v. 24, Lightfoot asserts, "St. Paul would have been the last to say that [Christians] bear their part in the atoning sacrifice of Christ."[67] Caird agrees and cites Paul's words in Rom 6:10 that Christ died "once for all."[68] Lohse also comments, that this "cannot be taken to mean that there still might be something lacking in the vicarious sufferings of Christ."[69] Dunn comments, "The words have caused bewilderment to generations of translators

---

66. Textual note. In 1:24 some MSS read "my" suffering (Sinaiticus3) but the text is otherwise agreed. In 1:27 "which" (*ho*, neuter gender) agrees with "mystery" and is supported by Alexandrinus and Vaticanus, but Sinaiticus, C, and D read *hos* (masculine) in agreement with "Christ." The UBS text reads *ho*. In 2:2 there are several variant readings, but "God, namely Christ" (Gk, *tou theou, Christou*) is graded as "almost certain" by UBS Committee (Metzger, *A Textual Commentary on the Greek New Testament*, 555).

67. Lightfoot, cited by Moule, *Colossians*, 75.

68. Caird, *Paul's Letters from Prison*, 184.

69. Lohse, *Colossians and Philemon*, 69.

and commentators."[70] O'Brien observes, "This verse has been an exegetical crux since earliest times."[71] However, Caird also adds, "The theme of joy in the face of suffering is common throughout the New Testament (e.g. Matt. 5:12; Acts 5:41; Heb. 10:34). It is enough for the servant that he be treated as his master (Matt. 10:24–26)."[72] Douglas Moo similarly comments, "V. 24b is one of the more difficult passages in the letter. . . . Paul highlights the corporate solidarity that Christ's people enjoy with him."[73]

Moo discusses five main possibilities for the meaning of "fill up"/"make up" what is left over in the afflictions of Christ,[74] but we shall just consider the two key approaches. Many argue that Christ's sufferings on the cross are necessarily shared by Christians, who are "in Christ." "What is lacking" could mean "what is yet to be shared." The double compound (Gk, *antanaplērō*), Caird argues, suggests that Paul suffers in some sense in place of the readers. Wesley comments, "That which remains to be suffered by his members."[75]

Others suggest what could be called "the apocalyptic view," that the corporate Christ or messianic community is destined to share a "quota" of sufferings before the purposes of God are complete. Dunn considers its connection with the messianic tribulation expected before the new age, alluding to Rom 8:18–23.[76] The idea of "messianic afflictions" may derive from Jewish apocalyptic, and at first sight may seem remote from Paul, but Martin

70. Dunn, *Colossians and Philemon*, 114.

71. O'Brien, *Colossians*, 75.

72. Caird, *Paul's Letters from Prison*, 184.

73. Moo, *Colossians and Philemon*, 150.

74. Moo and McKnight both cite the extensive work on the history of the exegesis of this difficult passage by Jacob Kremer, "Was an den Bedrängnissen des Christus Mangelt"; cf. Moo, *Colossians and Philemon*, 150; and McKnight, *Letter to the Colossians*, 187.

75. Wesley, *Colossians*, 15.

76. Lohse, *Colossians and Philemon*, 71; Dunn, *Colossians and Philemon*, 115. Bertram discusses "woes of the Messiah" in Kittel's article on "woes" (*ōdin*) (Bertram, "*ōdin*"). Lincoln also considers this suggestion (*Colossians*, 613).

comments that he bends it to his purpose, and the "quota" concept arises because "God sets a limit to these sufferings."[77] Lohse explains the notion of "quota" is "a definite measure for the last days." McKnight sets out the view as follows: "There was an appointed number of sufferings in the 'messianic woes' or exilic conditions of Israel (e.g. Dan. 7:21–22, 25–27; 12:1–3; Hab. 3:15; Zeph. 1:15; Mark 13:5–8; Matt. 24:4–8; Luke 21:8–11), so Christ absorbed many or most of them, but some suffering yet remains."[78]

This view is in harmony with several passages in 2 Corinthians: "As the sufferings (Gk, *ta pathēmata*) of Christ abound in you" (1:5); "we are always being given up to death for Jesus' sake, so that the life of Jesus may be made visible in our mortal flesh. So death is at work in us, but life in you" (4:11–12). O'Brien cites the parallel in 2 Cor 1:3–11. Dunn refers to "Christian existence as a lifelong process in which dying with Christ leads to a share in his final resurrection (Rom. 6:5; Gal. 2:19)."[79] He adds, "Paul is clearly building on this theme." O'Brien suggests that "sufferings of Christ" could be "a genitive of quality" referring to sufferings which resemble those of Christ."[80] Photius, Theodoret, and Pelagius, took this view. On the basis of the double compound *antanplērō* Robertson suggests that first Jesus had his "turn" in bearing the corporate sufferings of the messianic community, then Paul had had his "turn" (a metaphor from cricket or baseball), and finally other believers will participate in those afflictions. However, *the sufferings of Jesus alone were expiatory.*[81] Nevertheless, "Christ continues to suffer in his members, not least in Paul himself."[82]

McKnight considers "the apocalyptic or eschatological view" of v. 24 to be in some ways "the most attractive theory." It is certainly popular with scholars, with Peter O'Brien, N. T. Wright, Murray Harris, Marianne Meye Thompson, David Pao, and others

77. Martin, *Colossians*, 70.
78. McKnight, *Letter to the Colossians*, 188.
79. Dunn, *Colossians and Philemon*, 115.
80. O'Brien, *Colossians*, 77.
81. Robertson, *Word Pictures in the New Testament*, vol. 4, 484.
82. O'Brien, *Colossians*, 80.

broadly supporting it. Yet for McKnight, "this very popular view seems to strain Paul's [eschatology]. For this view to work, Paul has to think that the messianic woes have not yet been completed. . . . But against this view is that Jesus was raised to end the messianic woes. In his death he defeated suffering and death itself. [It is] the far side of the resurrection."[83] While the apocalyptic view has much to commend it, McKnight's caution is wise. He rightly lays the emphasis on Paul and other Christians sharing Christ's mission. McKnight concludes, "A more eclectic approach is required, one that might clumsily be called *the missional-Christological theory*—namely that Paul understands his gospel-mission sufferings as an intentional entrance into the sufferings of, or like those of, Christ."[84] Moule also defends a hybrid approach: "I am inclined to believe that the two [views] should be combined, although the second is more uniformly probable and is the dominant idea."[85] That is to say, he recommends combining the idea of the "quota of sufferings" with the general notion of "sharing Christ's sufferings."

Here in Colossians "in my flesh" is rendered by the NEB "in my poor human flesh." This is probably correct. Although "flesh" in Paul often denotes more, he can use it simply to speak of humans in their weakness and vulnerability. Lincoln writes, "The combination of the twofold designation as servant with the stress on Paul's sufferings in 1:24 recalls the Suffering Servant figure from Isaiah 40–55."[86] Calvin affirms that this verse depends on "so great a unity between Christ and his members."[87]

"According to the responsibility (Gk, *kata tēn oikonomian*) given by God" in v. 25 might be rendered "according to the dispensation [or economy, administration, or stewardship] of God," according to Robertson. In Caird's view this means simply "the

83. McKnight, *Letter to the Colossians*, 189.

84. McKnight, *Letter to the Colossians*, 189 (his italics). He also cites Settler, "An Interpretation of Colossians 1:24 in the Framework of Paul's Mission."

85. Moule, *Colossians*, 76.

86. Lincoln, *Colossians*, 614.

87. Calvin, *Philippians, Colossians, and Thessalonians*, 164.

task assigned by God."[88] To "fulfil" or "to make fully completed" (Gk, *plērōsai*) means "to give full scope to the Word of God." Paul's near parallel occurs in Rom 15:19, where he speaks of "bringing to completion" the ministry of the Word, having in view his mission in Spain. 2 Timothy 4:17 is also relevant: "that through me the gospel may be fully proclaimed (Gk, *plērophoreō*)." Once again we may cite John Collins' recent research on *diakonos* (minister), which showed that a "minister" was primarily one who deputized for a presbyter and could perform the same ministerial function.[89] Dunn warns us that the term does not yet have a uniform function. This verse confirms that the main function is ministering the Word. Paul is a minister according to the plan of God.

(b) Paul's message (1:26–29)

Margaret MacDonald comments on v. 26, "The concepts of mystery (Gk, *mystērion*), to hide (Gk, *apokryptō*), and to reveal (Gk, *phaneroō*) reflect a revelation formula or schema (what was previously hidden is now proclaimed publicly) which occurs repeatedly in Pauline literature. This schema may well draw its origins from a ritual setting where the contrast between one's past life and one's new life was experienced and celebrated (cf. 1 Cor. 2:6–16; Rom. 16:25–27; 1 Tim. 3:16."[90] For Paul himself, the "mystery" referred to was primarily the admissions of the gentiles to sharing God's salvation. Outside Paul, the term *mystērion* meant many possible things in the Greek and Oriental world, including the mystery cults. There it usually denoted secret teaching, on the attainment of salvation, often by association with a particular deity.[91] The significance of the mystery religions for Colossians, however, has more recently been questioned, not least because of the later dating

---

88. Caird, *Paul's Letters from Prison*, 185.

89. Collins, *Diakonia*.

90. MacDonald, *Colossians Ephesians*, 81.

91. Cf. Reitzenstein, *Hellenistic Mystery Religions*.

of many of the mystery religions. Seeing the ideas of mystery religions in Colossians may well be anachronistic.

It is more helpful to see a correspondence between the Greek term for "mystery" and the Aramaic *rāz*, secret, as found in Daniel (2:18, 19, 27–30, 47), where it denotes an eschatological mystery concealed in the present but suggesting ordained future events. It may denote things that must come to pass, which are partially revealed now. Paul uses the word some twenty-one times in his letters. Primary passages include 1 Cor 2:6–10 and Rom 10:25–27. Paul's emphatic "but now" (Gk, *nun de*) emphasizes the apocalyptic shift that has taken place with the mystery of gentile inclusion now being revealed to Christian believers in the present. Paul uses three Greek words to convey this: being revealed (Gk, *apokalyptō*), becoming known (*gnōrizō*), and being made manifest (*phaneroō*). These three expressions of revelation take place in Paul's apostolic preaching.

"The riches of the glory of this mystery" in v. 27 is a typical Pauline use of the metaphor of inexhaustible treasure. The inclusion of the gentiles is, for Paul, the crowning glory of the mystery, as we have noted (Gk, *to ploutos tēs doxēs tou mystēriou toutou*). He keenly feels the high honor of performing this task. "Glory" is used many times by Paul of the glory of God, where it derives from the Hebrew *kābōd*, which refers to the splendor of the glorious presence of God. In origin the word had to do with being weighty, in the sense of having *gravitas*.

Moule associates "glory" with the *Shekinah*, or indwelling presence of God. He comments, "It carried with it the associations of visible light and splendour (as does 'brilliance' in its metaphorical sense); but especially as a result of the Incarnation, the essential splendour came to be recognised as a moral splendour—the glorious life of service lived by Christ and laid down for others in the crucifixion."[92] Hence, Moule continues, the *Shekinah* glory of the life of Christ is to be seen at its most brilliant when he is washing his disciples feet (John 13:1–11), or has reached the hour of death.

92. Moule, *Colossians and Philemon*, 83.

Barth similarly argues that the glory of God is often seen in his humility.[93]

Paul uses the word "glory" and its cognates more than eighty times. In Jesus Christ, God reveals the splendor of his presence. Caird comments, "Those who by faith were united with him were already acting as mirrors of his glory and undergoing a hidden transfiguration (2 Cor. 3:18) which would reach its culmination only with the return of Christ (Col. 3:4)." He adds that in Christ "Paul finds the brightest jewels in God's treasury of glory and the guarantee of his hopes for the future."[94] "Glory" is also associated with the humility of God in John's Gospel, as when "We beheld his glory" (John 1:14) refers to his being born as one of us in the incarnation.[95]

As Martin comments, much of Paul's apostolic task and method is summed up in v. 28 in the three words "proclaim" (Gk, *kataggellomen*), "warn" (Gk, *nouthetountes*), and "teach" (Gk, *didaskontes*).[96] Dunn observes that, given the cosmic context, "every single person" (Gk, *panta anthrōpon*)—the objects of Paul's mission—refers not simply to everyone in Colossae, but to everyone in a *universal* sense.[97]

In "to present everyone full-grown (Gk, *teleios*) in Christ" (v. 28), *teleios* is usually translated "mature" (NRSV, NEB) or "perfect" (NJB, NIV). In the case of sacrificial victims it means "without blemish," but otherwise means "complete," "whole," or "full-grown."[98] It may also mean "reaching the highest standard." This goal is not reserved for the elite but is within the grasp of everyone.

In v. 29, Paul shows that he includes himself in this ultimate aspiration, but also that it is not reached without toil and labor.

93. Barth, *The Humanity of God.*

94. Caird, *Paul's Letters from Prison*, 186.

95. Caird, "The Glory of God in the Fourth Gospel."

96. Martin, *Colossians and Philemon*, 72.

97. Dunn, *Colossians and Philemon*, 125.

98. Danker, BDAG, 995–96.

Caird comments, "The toil is Paul's, but the energy is Christ's."[99] This well explains the Greek : *agōnizomenos kata tēn energeian autou*. Victor Pfitzner has shown in a volume entirely devoted to this subject how indispensable is the theme of struggling. He traces the analogy between Greek competitive games and struggle in the Christian life.[100] One close parallel is Phil 3:12–14.

(c) Paul's call to the church in Colossae (2:1–5)

Paul continues the theme of greatly striving or struggling in 2:1. Here he notes his own hard effort for the benefit of both the readers in Colossae and the Christians in Laodicea. We may also understand an implicit reference to Hierapolis to which Paul alludes in 4:13. These three centers made up the three main cities of the Lycus valley. This hard effort involved wrestling in prayer, thought, and sometimes anxiety. In 2 Cor 11:28 Paul acknowledges, "Besides other things, I am under daily pressure because of my anxiety for all the churches."

In v. 2, the goal of Paul's struggles is expressed in terms of the readers being encouraged, as Lincoln argues.[101] My translation "fully assured understanding" literally means in the Greek "the conviction that comes from understanding" (*tēs plērophorias tēs syneseōs*). Caird comments, "Paul is praying that the experience of being united in love will give them enough understanding to be the basis of a settled conviction, and that this in turn will lead to a grasp of God's larger purpose."[102] Robertson observes that this requires the full and balanced exercise of all one's mental powers.[103] Paul uses the word "I appeal" (Gk, *parakaleō*), which as Bjerkelund argues, can mean also "to ask" or "to beseech" and is often used

99. Caird, *Paul's Letters from Prison*, 187 (his italics).

100. Pfitzner, *Paul and the Agon Motif*.

101. Lincoln, *Colossians*, 616.

102. Caird, *Paul's Letters from Prison*, 187.

103. Robertson, *Word Pictures in the New Testament*, vol. 4, 488.

as a formula to introduce pastoral administration in letters.[104] But "comfort" is also an acceptable translation. "Hearts" here denotes the inner life or core of a person.

"All the treasures of wisdom and knowledge" (2:3) translates Greek "*pantes hoi thēsauroi tēs sophias kai gnōseōs.*" All this is found, not in secret mysteries, but in Christ. *He* is our treasure and storehouse. All the powers and activities formerly attributed in Jewish traditions to the personified wisdom of God must now be attributed to Christ.[105] This phrase is not a quotation, but a loose reflection of Isa 45:3. Wright comments, "Christ sums up in himself all that the Jews predicated of Wisdom (cf. Prov. 2:1–8). . . . Christ himself is 'the mystery of God.'"[106]

Verse 4 immediately explains Paul's point: nobody is to deceive the readers with plausible arguments into thinking that something further than Christ is still needed. Christ *alone* is utterly sufficient for the desires and needs of the readers.

The metaphor of "unbroken order" (Gk, *taxin*) and reference to "steadfastness" or "firmness" (Gk, *stereōma*) in v. 5 were military images denoting orderly array. The church in Colossae was to present a firm front against all seductive teaching. Paul's allusion here to being absent in body but present in spirit is closely parallel with his comment in 1 Cor 5:3.

Questions for reflection on 1:24—2:5

1. Does Paul's language about "making up, in turn, what is lacking in the afflictions of Christ" (v. 24) contradict "God has rescued you from the power of darkness and transferred us into the kingdom of his beloved Son" (1:13)? If not, what does "what is lacking" mean?

104. Bjerkelund, *Parakalō*.
105. Caird, *Paul's Letters from Prison*, 187.
106. Wright, *Colossians and Philemon*, 99.

2. Do we rejoice if we are suffering for the benefit of the gospel or of the church? How does such suffering share in Christ's suffering?

3. Can anyone aspire to be servants of the church, or are we servants only if God calls us to this task? Whom does God call?

4. What especially does Paul mean by the "mystery"? Why is it such an incredible wonder to him?

5. Which three activities characterize the apostolic proclamation of the gospel? Do we value all three equally?

6. Is it our aim to be presented "full-grown" to Christ? What else might "full-grown" mean? What might help us to reach this goal?

7. What place does struggle occupy in our lives? Do we try to escape struggle in favor of suggesting that Christians should aim only at peace? Is "struggle" positive or negative?

8. Should we try to struggle for churches other than our local church?

9. How can we best aim at applying all our mental capacities to understanding knowledge of God and resisting plausible seductions?

10. Is the church as a whole "ordered and steady"? Why does Paul use military imagery here?

3. Confrontation with opponents: the power of the risen Christ (2:6–15)

> 6 As therefore you received Christ Jesus as Lord, go on walking in him, 7 rooted and built up in him and firmly established in your faith, as you have been taught, abounding in thanksgiving. 8 Take heed lest anyone captivates you through his philosophy and vain deceit derived from human tradition according to the principles of the world, and not according to Christ. 9 For in him

dwells all the fullness of the Godhead in bodily form.
10 You are given "fullness" in Christ, who is the head
over all sovereignty and ruling forces. 11 In him you
received a circumcision not made with human hands
but in the putting off of the body of the old nature. This
is the circumcision of Christ. 12 You were buried with
him in baptism and raised with him through faith in the
power of God who raised him from the dead. 13 And
you who were dead through your trespasses and through
your being physically uncircumcised he has brought to
life with him, having forgiven us all our trespasses. 14
He has cancelled the certificate of debt which was against
us. He has taken it out of the way, nailing it to the cross.
15 He disarmed the principalities and powers, making a
public show of them, triumphing over them in Christ.[107]

In Andrew Lincoln's words, these verses make it clear that orthodoxy and orthopraxis go hand in hand.[108] This section (2:6–15)
is full of Greek terms that call for abundant explanations. In v. 6
"you received" (Gk, *parelabete*) is one of the standard terms for the
transmission and reception of a tradition, as in 1 Cor 11:23 and
15:1.[109] There Paul also uses "handing on" (Gk, *paradidōmi*). The
Greek translated "go on walking" is a present continuous indicative (Gk, *peripateite*). The use of the repeated "the" in v. 6—literally, *"the* Christ Jesus *the* Lord"—occurs nowhere else in Paul. As
against the so-called gnostics, this may call attention to the historical Jesus, to the particular Christ or Messiah, and his sovereign

107. Textual note. In v. 7 the UBS committee favors the reading that we
render "your faith" (Gk, *tē pistei*), which is supported by B, D*, 33, and others. It takes account of other readings (Metzger, *A Textual Commentary on the
Greek New Testament*, 555). Also in the same verse "in thanksgiving" (Gk, *en
eucharistia*) is described by the UBS Committee as "almost certain," regarding
a longer reading as due to a copyist's assimilation. In v. 13b there is a little
uncertainty about the readings "you" (Gk, *hymin*) and "us" (Gk, *hēmin*) in
"forgiven us all our trespasses." But "us" is supported by Þ46, B, 33, and other
MSS. The UBS committee graded "us" as "certain," noting the similarity of the
vowels "u" and "ē" in pronunciation (ibid., 556).

108. Lincoln, *Colossians*, 620.

109. Dunn, *Colossians and Philemon*, 138; Abbott, *Ephesians and Colossians*, 244.

Lordship. The names occur also in Gal 5:24 and 6:12. We could equally translate: "Jesus as Christ (Messiah) and Lord," although this is less likely.[110]

Lincoln points out that v. 7 contains four participles conveying imagery of the readers' relation to their Lord.[111] The word for "rooted" (Gk, *errizōenoi*) derives from *riza*, root, and is a perfect passive participle. Paul then changes the image from the metaphor of a growing tree to a solidly founded building: "rooted and built up," as in 1 Cor 3:10 and 12. "And firmly established" translates the Greek *bebaioumenoi* from *bebaioō*, to make firm or stable. "As you were taught" underlines the firm tradition of apostolic truth, which had been transmitted to them.

The readers must not be captured by mere human tradition (2:8). "Take heed" translates the Greek *blepete*. This has the force of "look out," "see to it," or "beware"; "lest anyone that captivates you" translates a negative purpose. "Captivates" translates the Greek *ho sylagōgōn*, which is a verb from later Greek in the form of a participle, and derives from *sylē*, booty, with *agō* to lead or carry (i.e., to carry off a slave as booty, or "to captivate," as NJB).[112] NJB also admirably conveys the precise sense of v. 8b: "with the empty lure of a philosophy of the kind that human beings hand on, based on the principles of this world and not on Christ." But this might perhaps over-translate, or go slightly beyond, the Greek.

The phrase "the principles of the world," however, is a fair translation of the controversial Greek *stoicheia*. *Stoichos* originally meant anything in a row or series, like the letters of an alphabet or the materials from which the universe was made, but it later became a word for "elementary teaching," and eventually passed into gnostic vocabulary for its own philosophy. The NRSV translates this as "the elemental spirits of the universe."[113] We must, all the

---

110. Moule, *Colossians and Philemon*, 89.

111. Lincoln, *Colossians*, 620.

112. Danker, BDAG, 955; Moule, *Colossians and Philemon*, 90; Caird, *Paul's Letters from Prison*, 189–91.

113. Danker, BDAG, 946; Lohse, *Colossians and Philemon*, 96–99.

same, heed James Barr's warning that sometimes etymology suggests more about a word's history than about its present meaning.

Douglas Moo considers three main meanings of the Greek *stoicheia*. He writes, (1) "In Paul's day (and after) the word was most often used to denote the 'fundamental components' of the universe, the 'elements' from which all matter was composed— usually identified as air, earth, fire, and water. The word is used in this sense in its three LXX occurrences (4 Macc. 12:13; Wis. 7:17; 19:18) in most of its occurrences in Philo, Josephus, and the apostolic fathers, and in two of the six New Testament occurrences (2 Pet. 3:10, 12)."[114] (2) He continues: the word is also used in the sense of the "essential principles" of a particular area of study. This meaning is also found in the New Testament (in Heb 5:12).[115] (3) Finally, he writes, "Stoicheia came to be used for spiritual beings. . . . Its first extant use in this way comes in the post-NT *Testament of Solomon*" (cosmic rulers of darkness, in 18:2).[116] He concludes that each of these meanings has strong lexical evidence and support among writers, although the third meaning is most fashionable today. It is these "rulers" who might enslave the Colossians. On the other hand, there is no solid evidence of this use of *stoicheia* "until the third century A.D."[117]

We must take seriously, Moo argues, the ancient worldview. He writes that "*stoicheia* as a reference to spiritual beings would have been an easy one in the context of the ancient worldview. . . . Hence many commentators speak here in Colossians of 'astral spirits.'"[118] Then to be taken captive would mean to be in bondage to astral spirits. Yet, Moo argues, "There is no evidence that the word *stoicheia* was used to refer to spiritual beings until the third century A.D." By contrast, the material components of the universe were often associated with spiritual beings or the gods. He appeals to Philo for the tendency of the Greeks to divinize the material

114. Moo, *Colossians and Philemon*, 187–88.

115. Moo, *Colossians and Philemon*, 188.

116. Moo, *Colossians and Philemon*, 188.

117. Moo, *Colossians and Philemon*, 189.

118. Moo, *Colossians and Philemon*, 189.

elements (e.g., *On the Decalogue* 53; *On the Contemplative Life*, 3). This "philosophy" becomes virtually a diffused pantheism.[119]

"Through philosophy" (Gk, *dia tēs philosophias*) does not mean "philosophy" in the traditional, normal, or modern sense of the word. Paul does not condemn philosophy as such, but specifically what the false teachers called their system of thought. Harris writes, "Paul means neither philosophy in general nor classical Greek philosophy specifically but so-called philosophy" (to use the term of the false teachers).[120] In Paul's day, "rhetoric" (of a certain type) was a more pressing danger to Christian faith than traditional philosophy.

O'Brien points out, "The evil powers which are seen to be behind the false practices and regulations (2:20) have been defeated and publicly disgraced in Christ."[121] He also reminds us, as others do, that here Paul uses the catch-words of his opponents' "philosophy." Scot McKnight argues that this "human-centered" tradition has doctrinal, spiritual, and cosmological aspects, citing a wide range of ancient and modern writers.[122]

The word translated "Godhead" (Gk, *theotētos*) in v. 9 may equally well be translated "deity" or "divinity." This verse takes up what was said about "fullness" in 1:15–20. It is clear that in Christ dwells all "the fullness" (Gk, *to plērōma*) of God, but "in bodily form" (Gk, *sōmatikōs*, bodily) is open to four interpretations. Caird lists these as (i) "in bodily form, i.e., incarnate"; or (ii) "embodied, i.e., in the corporate life of the church"; or (iii) "in organic unity, and not diffused throughout a hierarchy of powers"; or (iv) "in solid reality."[123] It is possible to add (v) "actually" or "in reality," as favored by Augustine, and (vi) "in essence," as favored by most Greek fathers and Calvin.[124]

119. Moo, *Colossians and Philemon*, 190–93.

120. Harris, *Colossians and Philemon*, 92.

121. O'Brien, *Colossians, Philemon*, 137.

122. McKnight, *Letter to the Colossians*, 227; cf. Schweizer, "Slaves of the Elements and Worshipers of Angels"; Smith, *Heavenly Perspective*.

123. Caird, *Paul's Letters from Prison*, 191.

124. Moule, *Colossians and Philemon*, 92.

Lightfoot and (with qualifications) Moule support the first alternative, while Caird dismisses it on the ground that Christ's supremacy over the powers comes only with the resurrection and that the incarnation is not a process of filling but of self-emptying. The second suggestion may have some attractiveness, but it places too much weight on the adverb, and looks like an obscure anticipation of what is said more clearly in the next verse. The third proposal has similar objections. Caird comments that this might be possible if the term "fullness" is taken from the vocabulary of Paul's opponents, but of this we cannot be certain. Chrysostom and Theodore of Mopsuestia apparently favored this, but Paul does not use the word "body" of the universe, and the fullness of deity is something more than the lordship over the universe. The fourth proposal is Caird's favored explanation, especially in the light of v. 17, "where *soma* (body) is used to denote the solid reality of the new-age in contrast with the shadowy anticipation of it in the legal systems of the age that is past."[125]

On the whole, "in concrete visible form" or "incarnate" seems the simplest and most probable interpretation. Dunn calls this "the encounterable reality of the indwelling."[126] Lohse concludes that the word "bodily" simply suggests that "the divine indwelling is real."[127]

"You are made full in Christ" in v. 10 emphasizes the *completeness* of the Christian's experience of Christ, who gives fullness of life. The false teachers had tried to persuade the Colossians that completeness was out of reach until they had observed the rules and regulations of the so-called gnostics. But Christ is the head over all "sovereignty and ruling forces." All other authority comes second after Christ.

The next two verses, 11–12, continue the theme of incorporation into Christ with particular reference to circumcision and baptism. "In whom you were circumcised" is parallel to "you were buried with him" in v. 12. The sudden introduction of circumcision

---

125. Moule, *Colossians and Philemon*, 192.

126. Dunn, *Colossians and Philemon*, 152.

127. Lohse, *Colossians and Philemon*, 100.

seems to be so unexpected that some have argued that it was a feature of the syncretism being taught by Paul's teachers. But, as Bruce declares, "the circumcision of Christ is not primarily circumcision as a Jewish infant of eight days old (Luke 2:21); it is rather his crucifixion, the 'putting off' of the body of the flesh, of which his literal circumcision was at best a token-anticipation."[128] Paul in v. 12 explicitly states that this is not a circumcision made with hands, i.e., it is a "spiritual circumcision" (NRSV). Lincoln comments, "Instead of talking about their union with Christ in his death, burial, and resurrection . . . as Paul does in Romans 6 . . . the writer speaks of their union with Christ in his circumcision, burial, and resurrection."[129] This is one of many examples where Lincoln doubts clear and decisive parallels with undisputed Pauline epistles.

"Buried with him in baptism and raised with him" (2:12) is broadly parallel to Rom 6:3–4. Baptism proclaims that the old order is past and over, and that we are united with Christ in his resurrection. In baptism we escape the jurisdiction in which world-rulers exercise their power. It belongs to Paul's theme of participation with Christ. Colossians 3:1 will expound this further. As elsewhere in Paul, God is the agent of Christ's resurrection, and God is also the agent of the resurrection of believers. Belief or faith in the possibility of resurrection is essentially belief or faith in God's power to bring it about. In Colossians, Paul says that Christians have *already been raised* with Christ (2:12). Many contrast this with the future resurrection in Romans 6. But Caird contests this, arguing that "will be" in Rom 6:5 is a logical rather than a chronological future (if A is true, then B will also be true).[130] He writes, "In all three letters [i.e., Romans, 2 Corinthians, and Philippians] union with Christ in death and resurrection is an objective reality offered and accepted in baptism, with consequences to be worked out in

---

128. Bruce, *Ephesians and Colossians*, 234.

129. Lincoln, Colossians, 623.

130. Caird, *Paul's Letters from Prison*, 194.

Christian experience and behaviour, and with an assurance of ultimate confirmation in the redemption of the body."[131]

"And *you*" (Gk, *kai hymeis*) in v. 13 is emphatic, implying "you
gentiles," "were dead through your trespasses" (Gk, *paraptōmasin*,
from *parapiptō*, to lapse or fall, also indicates going astray or trans-
gression). The second clause "through your being uncircumcised
in your bodies (*sarkos*)" underlines their status as gentiles. The two
clauses together indicate their former lost condition. They were
"dead" and alienated or separated from God as gentiles, as O'Brien
suggests.[132] But "he made alive with him" (Gk, *synezōopoiēsen*)
also takes an emphatic position. Dunn comments, "God (now the
subject) making alive the dead is another way of speaking of the
resurrection."[133]

"This he set aside, nailing it to the cross." The Greek of v. 14
may seem complex, but it becomes straightforward once the legal situation that Paul presupposes is fully understood. The verb
"he has cancelled" (Gk, *exaleipsas*) means "to rub out," "to erase,"
or "wipe off," but in a legal context the idea is best conveyed by
"cancel."

What has been cancelled by God? The Greek word *cheirogra-
phon* literally means "what was written by hand," but in this legal
context it denotes a promissory note made in the handwriting
of the signatory, often with a penalty clause.[134] Our translation,
"certificate of debt" intends to bring this out. Some translate it as
"bond." Caird explains:

> The idea is that the Jews had signed a contract to obey the
> law, and in their case the penalty for breach of contract
> was death (Deut. 27:14–26; 30:15–20). Paul assumes that
> the Gentiles were by conscience committed to a similar
> obligation to the moral law in so far as they understood it

131. Caird, *Paul's Letters from Prison*, 194.

132. O'Brien, *Colossians, Philemon*, 122.

133. Dunn, *Colossians and Philemon*, 162.

134. Danker, BDAG, 1083 is clear but brief; see Robertson, *Word Pictures
in the New Testament*, vol. 4, 494; and Deissmann, *Bible Studies*, 247; and Deissmann, *Light from the Ancient East*, 332.

> (cf. Rom. 2:14–15). Since the obligation had never been discharged, the bond [or promissory note] remained outstanding against us, with a constant threat that the penalty clause [i.e., of death] should be invoked.[135]

Thus, the bond stood against us. "Against us" (Gk, *hypenantios*) is a double compound adjective (*hypo+en+antios*), which is used in the New Testament only in Heb 10:27. Lincoln, however, argues that the background of the "document" is to be found in apocalyptic, in books of good and evil deeds, where a book of indictment could be held "against us" and then erased.[136] He cites such sources as Apoc. Zeph. 3:6–9; 7:1–8, but although almost convincing, Caird's explanation from the Old Testament (see above) seems less speculative.

McKnight explains that "nailing it to the cross" (v. 14) does not imply that two acts are performed, namely (i) erasing and (ii) taking away, but "one major act (new creation)" explored in various ways. This is clear, he says, because the cross is an instrument of punishment; indeed the "crime" was notified in the titulus on the cross as 'King of the Jews.'"[137]

The Greek word in v. 15 that we have translated as "disarmed" (*apekdysamenos*) also means "to strip off" or "to take off" (as at 3:9), but Danker and others favor "disarmed" or "despoiled" in this present context.[138] Many of the Greek fathers, and in modern times Lightfoot and O'Brien, suggest that the hostile forces clung to Jesus on the cross and were torn off and cast aside for ever.[139] Hanson argues that "made a public example" (Gk, *edeigmatisen en parresia*) means "showed them in their true character."[140] "Triumphing" occurs in 2 Cor 2:14. The image here and in 2 Corinthians is of the celebration of a military victory, in which a Roman general would

135. Caird, *Paul's Letters from Prison*, 195 (his italics).

136. Lincoln, *Colossians*, 625.

137. McKnight, *Colossians*, 250.

138. Danker, BDAG, 100.

139. Lightfoot, *Colossians and Philemon*, 188; O'Brien, *Colossians, Philemon*, 127.

140. Hanson, *Studies in Paul's Technique and Theology*, 10–11.

lead a conquered army in a victory parade.[141] Christ's triumph was won on the cross. Lightfoot comments, "The convict's gibbet is the victor's car [or carriage]."[142] Paul may be using a mixture of metaphors here, but he often does this. Moo points out that whereas in 2:10 Paul saw Christ's headship as due to his place over creation, here in v. 15 Christ is head because of the cross.[143] He acknowledges that *apekdysamenos*—"strip off" or "disarm"—causes differences of interpretation, but concludes that the sense is active, i.e., "he [Christ] stripped [clothes] from the powers and authorities" or disarmed them. He comments, "A key factor that is not always given due recognition is the personal object [i.e., the rulers and the powers] that follows the verb here."[144] Pao reaches the same conclusion.[145]

Questions for reflection

1. Even if we have "received" the apostolic tradition, how much still depends on our actively "going on" with the Christian life?

2. How does Paul's metaphor of "being rooted" complement and clarify the other metaphor of "being built up"? Why are both needed?

3. What things today are most likely to captivate Christians seductively by "principles of the world"? How does Paul's use of the term "philosophy" here differ from normal use?

4. If the God, whom we cannot see, revealed himself "bodily" in Jesus Christ, why do we complain that God sometimes seems distant or ill-defined?

141. Williamson, "Led in Triumph: Paul's Use of *Thriambeuō*."
142. Lightfoot, *Colossians and Philemon*, 188.
143. Moo, *Colossians and Philemon*, 212.
144. Moo, *Colossians and Philemon*, 213.
145. Pao, *Colossians and Philemon*, 172.

5. Why does Paul say that we are "given fullness" in Christ? Is this borrowing a term from his opponents? Or is it related to sufficiency and completion? Or is it both?

6. What today might we think of as "ruling forces," of which Christ is head?

7. What do those of us who are gentile readers make of spiritual circumcision? Why is baptism a sign of "putting off" and "putting on"?

8. For gentiles, how does the Jewish "certificate of debt" [NRSV, "record that stood against us"] affect us?

9. What has "cancelling," "erasing," and "forgiving" to do with nailing our obligations to the cross?

10. How does God's triumph relate to Christ's "making a public example or show" of principalities and powers (or rulers and authorities) on the cross?

4. Guard your freedom, or Christian liberty from the Jewish law (2:16–23)

16 Accordingly do not let anyone pass judgment on you in matters of food and drink or in taking part in feasts and new moons or sabbaths. 17 These are only a shadow of things to come, the substance belongs to Christ. 18 Do not let anyone disqualify you by delighting in voluntary self-abasement and worship of angels, taking his stand on his visions, puffed up without cause, by his all-too-human mind; 19 not holding fast to the head, from whom the body, supplied and knit together through its joints and ligaments, increases with the increase that comes from God.

20 If with Christ you died to the principles of the world, why do you live under the regulations of the world? 21 "Do not handle, do not taste, do not touch." 22 All these regulations are to perish as we use them, but they are simply human commands and teachings. 23

These things have a reputation of wisdom in promoting self-imposed piety and humility and unsparing treatment of the body but are not of any value in checking indulgence of the flesh.[146]

(a) Freedom in respect to food and festivals (2:16–17)

Caird comments, "Unfortunately this is one of the most obscure paragraphs he [Paul] ever wrote."[147] Perhaps, he adds, this is because he is quoting from the jargon used by the false teachers. The unusual complexity of the Greek means that many Greek words deserve comment, as they are capable of more than one meaning.

Lohse writes, "In the ancient world the view was widespread that by asceticism and fasting man served the deity, came closer to him, or could prepare himself to receive the divine revelation."[148] Paul tells the readers that no one should sit in judgment on them[149] about what they choose to eat or drink. Paul is probably referring to strict ascetical regulations about refraining from meat and wine. In v. 17 he is attacking those false teachers who are "bursting with the futile conceit of worldly minds" (NEB). In the contrasting pair of words "shadow" (Gk, *skia*) and "substance" (Gk, *sōma*), the substance "is" Christ. Lohse observes, "The relationship between copy and original probably also played a role in the teaching of the Colossian 'philosophy.'"[150] Quite possibly, but the major concern is that of Christian eschatology. Wright comments, "These things [i.e., Jewish regulations] were a preparation for Christ's new age."[151]

---

146. Textual note: There are diverse readings in 2:13 and 23, but both are hardly relevant to the English. In v. 23 "and" is doubtful in the Greek. Many assume that a copyist inserted the word. The UBS Committee, however, regarded the omission of "and" as accidental, and supported its inclusion, following Sinaiticus, A, and C.

147. Caird, *Paul's Letters from Prison*, 196.

148. Lohse, *Colossians and Philemon*, 115.

149. J. B. Phillips has "criticize them."

150. Lohse, *Colossians and Philemon*, 116.

151. Wright, *Colossians and Philemon*, 123.

In v. 18 older commentators (such as Lightfoot) understood "rob you of your prize" to be derived from Gk, *brabeuō,* prize, but Caird insists on translating "disqualify" because the Greek word is derived from *brabeus,* umpire, where it means "to act as umpire against one," i.e., to disqualify (AV/KJV, NRSV, and Wright).[152] Danker has "to rob you of your prize"; the NJB has "cheated of your prize"; and Robertson and Moule include both possible derivations.[153] MacDonald writes, "In ancient literature it refers to being robbed of a prize unjustly. . . . Here the prize under dispute is clearly salvation."[154]

Moule writes, "The theosophic ritualist declares the Pauline opponent to be no genuine competitor in the race at all."[155] "What you eat or drink" probably refers to *kosher* laws of the Old Testament, which had been extended by Paul's time to include wine (cf. Lev 10:9 and Num 6:3). Whether we understand "shadow" in the Platonic sense of not-fully-real, or the eschatological sense of "a shadow of things to come," solid fulfilment is in Christ alone. This fulfilment has nothing to do with material things.

(b) Freedom in respect to asceticism and angel-worship (2:18–19)

In v. 18 "delighting in" (Gk, *thelōn en*) occurs here only once in the New Testament, but is defended by Lightfoot and others.[156] The JB has "people who like groveling to angels and worshipping them," and the NJB, "anyone who chooses to grovel to angels and worship them, pinning their hope on visions received." Caird paraphrases Lightfoot as follows: "There was an officious parade of humility in selecting these lower beings as intercessors, rather than appealing

152. Lightfoot, *St Paul's Epistles to the Colossians and to Philemon,* 195; Caird, *Paul's Letters from Prison,* 198.

153. Danker, BDAG, 515; Robertson, *Word Pictures in the New Testament,* vol. 4, 496; Moule, *Colossians and Philemon,* 103.

154. MacDonald, *Colossians, Ephesians,* 111.

155. Moule, *Colossians and Philemon,* 104.

156. Lightfoot, *St. Paul's Epistles to the Colossians and Philemon,* 195.

directly to the throne of grace."[157] Caird also understands "worship of angels" to be "Paul's contemptuous dismissal of their [i.e. the false teachers'] practices." He adds, "In their veneration for the most stringent rules that can be derived from the Old Testament they are really directing their worship to the angels through whom the law was given (Acts 7:53; Gal. 3:19; Heb. 2:2)." Calvin affirms on the one hand that "superstitious people" have always worshipped angels, which is wrong, but notes on the other hand that we must still honor angels.[158]

"Taking his stand on his visions" means depending on these imagined revelations. Lightfoot proposed "treading on empty air," suggesting the Greek, *eōra kenembateuōn*.[159] Moule similarly suggests, "walking upon the insubstantial ground of his visions."[160] Caird observes, "Taking his stand on visions is as good a guess as any at the meaning of three words which have so baffled the commentators that many have resorted to conjectural imitation. The difficulty is that this rendering does not exactly fit any of the attested meanings of the verb. On the other hand the attested meanings yield no tolerable sense."[161]

At a more immediately practical level Bruce comments, "Some people love to make a parade of exceptional piety. . . . They pretend to have found the way to a higher plane of spiritual experience, as though they had been initiated into sacred mysteries which gave them an infinite advantage over the uninitiated. Naturally this kind of claim impresses those who always fall for the idea of an 'inner ring.'"[162] "All-too-human outlook" or "sensual outlook" translates the Greek *tou noos tēs sarkos autou*, which Moule calls "an impossible phrase if taken literally—'his physical mind.'"[163]

157. Caird, *Paul's Letters from Prison*, 199.
158. Calvin, *Philippians, Colossians, and Thessalonians*, 196.
159. Lightfoot, *St. Paul's Epistles to the Colossians and Philemon*, 197.
160. Moule, *Colossians and Philemon*, 106.
161. Caird, *Paul's Letters from Prison*, 199.
162. Bruce, *Ephesians and Colossians*, 246.
163. Moule, *Colossians and Philemon*, 106.

Commenting on v. 19, Bruce writes, "This self-inflation and pride in private religious experiences comes of not maintaining contact with the head."[164] He adds that every part of the body will function properly so long as it is under the control of the head. But if it acts independently, consequences can be distressing. The application of the metaphor to "not holding fast the head" (Gk, *ou kratōn tēn kephalēn*), i.e., the headship of Christ, remains accurate, even if physiology of Paul's day had not fully worked out the role of the head. The headship of Christ is a major theme of this epistle. "Knit together" (Gk, *synbibazomenon*) is a continuous present passive participle, which, combined with "joints and ligaments," underlines this point.[165] The body exhibits a wonderful harmony *if united under the head*. Increase comes with the increase that comes from God.

(c) Freedom means death with Christ (2:20–23)

In vv. 11–12 Paul has already told the readers that they shared in the death of Christ and were "buried with him in baptism." Caird calls this "a vicarious, corporate death."[166] Christ died as the representative of all humanity. Christian believers now accept Christ's death as a representative event, which was undergone in their name. In baptism they make Christ's death their own. The corollary to this is that with Christ believers have died to the principles of this world. They have therefore also died to the world's regulations. They are no longer under any obligation to take the world's orders. This verse confirms the finality of the community's death-with-Christ. Death severs the bond that binds a slave to his master. Christians are no longer bound to the service of principalities and powers or service to the world.

The regulations of the world appear to be completely negative ones: "Do not handle, do not taste, do not touch" (2:21). Bruce

---

164. Bruce, *Ephesians and Colossians*, 251.

165. Aristotle and Galen use these physiological terms.

166. Caird, *Paul's Letters from Prison*, 201.

suggests that there may be a stage in a child's development when he or she must be told not to do this and not to touch that, but when he or she comes to years of discretion he or she can look at life from a more responsible angle and do what is proper without having to conform to a list of prohibitions that are suitable only for the years of infancy.[167] Merely negative rules do not avail for the maintenance and the growth of Christian life.

McKnight describes these rules as "what is probably a sarcastic list of three terms, each confirming again the Jewishness of the religion of the opponents: 'Do not handle! Do not taste! Do not touch!' The negations reveal a focus on ascetic denials designed to stimulate religious visions, mystical experiences, and special revelation."[168] The three items, he says, clarify the *stoicheia* as describing what in Paul's view mattered most to the opponents. We have no compelling explanation of any difference between "Do not handle!" (Gk, *mē hapsē*) and "Do not touch!" (Gk, *mēde thigēs*). It is just possible, McKnight adds, that "Do not touch!" may indicate not touching what is sacred (Exod 19:12) or prohibited (Lev 5:3). These might relate to halakic food laws or purity laws.

According to v. 22, these commandments, presumably suggested by the false teachers, are to perish "with the using of them" (Gk, *estin eis phthoran tē apochrēsei*, i.e., they are for perishing in the using). "To perish" is the word for decay or decomposition. Lightfoot asks, "Why are you attributing an inherent value to things which are fleeting? You yourselves are citizens of eternity and yet your thoughts are absorbed in the perishable."[169]

These prohibitions carry with them a reputation for wisdom (v. 23), because they are associated in people's minds with the philosophical schools, such as the Pythagoreans, and they have a veneration which is cheaply acquired. The translation "reputation of wisdom" (Gk, *logon sophias*) is favored by Abbot, Robertson, Bruce, Moule, and possibly Lightfoot and Wright, over "appearance

---

167. Bruce, *Ephesians and Colossians*, 254.

168. McKnight, *Letter to the Colossians*, 283.

169. Lightfoot, *St Paul's Epistles to the Colossians and to Philemon*, 204.

of wisdom."[170] The teachers' reputation for wisdom partly came from their association with ascetic philosophical schools, but it still remains a *self*-made cult. The word translated "self-imposed piety" or "rigor of devotion" (Gk, *ethelothrēskia*) occurs nowhere else in Greek literature, and Moulton and Milligan suggest that Paul has coined the word on the analogy of compounds that already existed in Greek. The stress is on the voluntary nature of the observances. It means devotion beyond the line of duty. It offered to God an addition to his requirements for which he did not ask.

The Greek literally is "They are of no value against the indulgence of the flesh," but Martin renders, "They are of no value in checking the indulgence of the flesh." Wright concludes, "What looks like rigorous discipline is in fact a subtle form of self-indulgence. This involves reading most of the verse as a parenthesis: 'which are (though possessing a reputation of wisdom with their self-imposed worship, abject grovelling and harsh physical discipline, all to no value) merely a way of gratifying the flesh.'"[171]

Questions for reflection

1. Are we over-concerned about other people's opinions of us? How can we strike a balance between sensitivity to the scruples of others and letting the opinions of others dictate our conduct?

2. Can we lose sight of the ultimate purpose of rituals and ceremonies in such a way that the outward form dominates the inner meaning? Can ritual become too fussy?

3. How can we find the right middle path between devaluing the ministry of angels and exalting intermediate powers to the place of Christ as our God-appointed mediator?

170. Wright, *Colossians and Philemon*, 132, says, "possibly a reputation for"; Moule, *Colossians and Philemon*, 108.

171. Wright, *Colossians and Philemon*, 132.

4. Can supposed private revelations take precedence over public truth or the apostolic gospel? How can we listen carefully to the voice of God to us while preserving critical, common-sense judgement and respect of others?

5. How far does closeness to Christ determine whether our Christian community is genuinely "knit together"?

6. Do we really live out the consequences of dying with Christ? What would it mean for us to live out our baptism?

7. Can negative regulations come to dominate our ethical behavior? Can we become too childlike in our appreciation of laws and regulations?

8. In what sense can regulations perish in the very process of using them? Can we too easily mistake the commandments of human beings as the commandments of God?

9. Are we too easily attracted by the merits of "asceticism," or is our problem the opposite one of lack of self-discipline?

10. Do we rejoice in the Christian freedom with which Christ has made us free? Do we fully realize the consequences of dying and rising with Christ?

III

Practice

The Rule of Christ in Everyday Life

3:1—4:6

1. The new resurrection life: laying aside old behavior (3:1–11)

1 Since, then, you have been raised with Christ, seek those things that are above, where Christ is, seated on the right hand of God. **2** Keep on thinking about the things above, not the things that are on the earth. **3** For you died and your life is hidden together with Christ in God. **4** When Christ shall be manifested, you also together with him shall be manifested in glory.

5 Treat as dead, therefore, your earthly limbs: sexual vice, impurity, passion, evil desires, insatiable greed which is idolatry, **6** on account of which the wrath of God comes, **7** in which you once walked and used to live; **8** but now, as for you, lay aside all of them: anger, bad temper, malice, abusive language, obscene language from your mouth. **9** Stop lying to one another. You have laid aside the old with your old self, **10** and you have put on a new self that is being renewed with a view to full knowledge in accord with the image of his Creator. [11] Here there does not exist gentile and Jew, circumcision and uncircumcision, uncivilized, foreigner, slave and free person. There is only Christ: he is everything and in everything.[1]

(a) You were raised with Christ (3:1–4)

The Greek literally has "if" in v. 1 (*If* then you have been raised with Christ) but most modern versions rightly interpret this as causal, or assumed as true, not hypothetical. Because Christians have been raised with Christ, their interests are now centered in him, i.e., their minds, attitudes, ambitions, and whole outlook, as Bruce comments.[2] Lincoln writes that these verses are part of the theme of union with Christ.[3] Bruce adds that the world cannot see the readers' real life at present, just as it cannot see Christ. In Scott's words, "By rising with Christ his followers share in his mind and will. They enter a new world."[4] Believers' present experience of Christ is expressed in terms of their links with the heavenly realm (1 Cor 15:47–49; Gal 4:26; Phil 3:20). "Above" here is synonymous with heaven. Resurrection life is *heavenly* life.

Wright observes, "The outstanding feature of this part of the letter is the sharp contrast between the old life and the new, as described in 3:5–11 and 3:12–17. It is salutary to ponder the characteristics of the one for a while, to sense its whole mood and style of life, and then switch suddenly to the other."[5] "Above" signals

---

1. Textual note: In 3:6 some MSS read "upon the disobedient sons." Some versions include these words but in brackets, as Aland's Gk. text. The NRSV has "those who are disobedient" with a marginal note. NJB and NIV omit the doubtful phrase but include a marginal note. Phillips virtually includes the words, and AV/KJV includes them. It is assumed that a copyist included the genuine words of Eph 5:6, by unconscious familiarity with them.

2. Bruce, *Ephesians and Colossians*, 257.

3. Lincoln, Colossians, 637.

4. Scott, *Colossians, Philemon, and Ephesians*, 62.

5. Wright, *Colossians and Philemon*, 133.

where Christ currently is; it does not denote simply the immaterial world, as it would in Hellenistic dualism. Christianity is not an "other worldly" faith in the negative sense but values the physical universe. "Seek" (Gk, *zēteite*) implies "to concentrate on," "to consider," or "to search."

The word-order in the Greek of v. 1 underlines the comma in the NRSV, NJB, and our translation, as against the absence of a comma in the NAB, where "is" is wrongly construed with "is seated." Thus, it should be rendered ". . . above, where Christ is, seated on the right hand of God" and not "above, where Christ is seated at the right hand of God" (NAB). "Christ is" should be construed with the realm above. Wright and MacDonald make this point.[6]

Christ's being seated at God's right hand has long been known as his heavenly session. This exaltation of Christ was proclaimed in earliest Christianity. At his enthronement Christ received a dignity and status comparable with God's. The phrase "at the right hand of God" explicitly uses the words of Psalm 110, which elsewhere dominates the Epistle to the Hebrews, is used by Jesus in Mark 12:35–37, and featured in the preaching of the earliest church according to Acts (e.g., Peter's sermon on Pentecost, Acts 2:34–35).

McKnight comments, "In 'seated at right hand of God' we enter into the profundity of early Christian Christology . . . Christ rules at the right hand of the Father (Acts 2:33–36; 1 Cor. 15:25; Eph. 1:20; Heb. 1:3, 13; 10:12, 13; 1 Pet. 3:22; Rev. 3:21; 22:1–3) and from that location he also intercedes (Rom. 8:34; Heb. 7:25; 1 Pet. 3:22)."[7] R. McL. Wilson comments, "This . . . brings to our notice trends and tendencies in early Christian thinking which help towards the understanding of some later developments. . . . [But] if our author has indeed gone beyond Paul's own teaching, he has not gone very far."[8]

Life in Christ is "hidden," in contrast to the normal, visible, parts of life in which we share the same needs, share the same

6. MacDonald, *Colossians, Ephesians*, 127; Wright, *Colossians and Philemon*, 136.

7. McKnight, *Letter to the Colossians*, 292.

8. Wilson, *Colossians and Philemon*, 237.

limitations, and are subject to the same social and environmental pressures as others. Christ himself is now "hidden" in heaven. "Hidden" does not mean "absent." The First Epistle of John has a similar idea: "Now are we sons of God, and it does not yet appear what we shall be, but we know that when he shall appear we shall be like him" (1 John 3:2). Lincoln writes, "There is to be the eager determination to take advantage of what has been achieved for them, to 'seek' the genuine realm above."[9] The motivation for this "seeking" is christological: they are to pursue the things "above" because that is where Christ is.

Bruce observes, "The apostles knew very well that they were using figurative language when they spoke of Christ's exaltation thus; they no more thought of a location on a literal throne at a literal right hand of God then we do. The static impression made by conventional artistic representations of such a literal enthronement of Christ is quite different from the dynamic New Testament conception." He continues: "What the apostles understood by the enthronement and God's right hand is plain from other terms which they used to convey the same idea: Christ has been given 'the name which is above every name, that in the name of Jesus every knee should bow . . . and every tongue confess that Jesus Christ is Lord' (Phil 2:10–11)."[10]

The second verse repeats the theme of the first, except that the emphasis falls on the continuous process of thinking (Gk, *phroneite*). Martin has "Let your thoughts dwell on that higher realm."[11] Robertson comments, "It does matter what we think and we are responsible for our thoughts."[12] On the other hand, he adds, Paul does not say that we should never think about earthly or everyday things. The Christian has to keep his or her feet on the ground. Paul wants us to set our minds on things above not so as to avoid the nitty gritty of everyday life on earth but because looking to the exalted Christ provides the vantage point for seeing our lives

9. Lincoln, Colossians, 638.

10. Bruce, *Ephesians and Colossians*, 258–59.

11. Martin, *Colossians and Philemon*, 101.

12. Robertson, *Word Pictures in the New Testament*, vol.4, 500.

here and now in the right context and light. It gives new eyes and new priorities.

Lincoln comments, "The imperative amounts to an injunction to be heavenly minded rather than earthly minded."[13] For the "philosophy" Paul is confronting this entailed a cosmological dualism in which the upper realm was good because it was spiritual and immaterial, while the lower realm evil because it was physical and material. But Christian thought is controlled by Paul's "eschatological perspective and has an ethical dimension."[14] "Things on earth" refers not to material, embodied human life so much as to life in bondage to cosmic powers (2:8, 20) and the practices of the old humanity (3:5–9).

"What was once, no longer applies," Lohse comments on v. 3. "The old life has been put aside forever through the death which they died together with Christ."[15] "Hidden" may possibly be a reference to what is buried being hidden in the earth, but it is more likely that it underlines that no demonic power can break in to interfere. The believer's life is safely "hidden away." Present hiddenness is contrasted with future manifest glory. Believers are "in God" because they are in Christ.

"When Christ shall be manifested" (v. 4) is an indefinite temporal clause ("indefinite" means uncertain as to time) beginning with Greek *hotan* and construed with the passive subjunctive *phanerōthē*. Thus, "*Whenever* Christ is manifested." Other allusions to the final coming of Christ agree that no definite time can be predicted. But the joy of the final coming is certain. In Romans, Paul tells us that the whole creation eagerly awaits and expects Christ's coming. We may compare 1 John 3:2, "We know that when he is revealed, we shall be like him." In the Old Testament even the last judgment is awaited with joy, for this is the time when God shall put all things right. Psalm 96:10–13 provides a classic example: "He shall judge the peoples with equity. Let the heavens be glad, and let the earth rejoice. . . . Then shall all the trees of the

13. Lincoln, *Colossians*, 638.

14. Lincoln, *Colossians*, 638.

15. Lohse, *Colossians and Philemon*, 133.

forest sing for joy before the LORD; for he is coming, for he is coming to judge the earth."[16] Elsewhere Paul asserts that the transformation of believers' bodies in the final resurrection will be in conformity with Christ's glorious body (Phil 3:21). Christians will share with Christ the experience of resurrection, although Christ experienced it first in time. God will then raise us, just as he has raised Christ already. He will raise us to glory. "Glory" has a variety of meanings, but here it retains its basic Hebrew sense of "weighty" or "being or impressive in splendor or grandeur". As John declares, "What we will be has not yet been revealed. What we do know is this: when he is revealed, we will be like him" (1 John 3:2).

(b) Laying aside old behavior (3:5–11)

"Therefore" (v. 5), as Bruce and others remark, signals the logical transition between the "doctrinal" and "practical" sections of the letter.[17] "Treat as dead" renders "put to death" (Gk, *nekrōsate*), or mortify. The NJB has "Kill everything that is earthly." We are to treat as dead not our physical bodies as such, for Paul calls these the temple of the Holy Spirit (1 Cor 6:19), but the attitudes that characterize our former godless lives. Paul explains at once what he means by "your earthly limbs": namely "sexual vice, impurity, passion, evil desire, covetousness which is idolatry." The self is to be transformed. Our limbs or "members" (Gk, *ta melē*) can be instruments of wickedness. Calvin writes, "They are, therefore, our members, in as much as they in a manner stick close to us."[18] Moule comments, "One's own private desires and ambitions [are] sentenced to death."[19]

Scott points out that Paul lists the specific sins that the converts had practiced in their former lives "to make it plainer" that

---

16. Cf. Thiselton, *Life after Death*, 166–84.

17. Bruce, *Ephesians and Colossians*, 264.

18. Calvin, *Philippians, Colossians and Thessalonians*, 208.

19. Moule, *Colossians and Philemon*, 115.

now they have become radically new people.[20] This applies even though lists of virtues and vices were popular in the ancient world. MacDonald comments, "Such lists were common in the writings of Hellenistic philosophers and some Jewish writings, including the Dead Sea Scrolls (e.g., 1QS 4:2–12, 18–26)."[21] It is probable, however, that these kinds of lists were also common in early Christian catechetical teaching, and that Paul borrowed such lists from pre-Pauline tradition.[22]

Paul's list here has parallels in Rom 1:24, 26, 29–31; 12:1–13; Gal 5:13–26; Eph 4:31; 5:3–5, 6:14–17; 1 Thess 4:1–12; Heb 13:1–17; and 1 Pet 1:13—4:11. Paul mentions sexual immorality or fornication (Gk, *porneia*) in Gal 5:19 and 1 Cor 6:9. English versions render *porneia* as "sexual vice" (NJB), "fornication" (NRSV and AV/KJV), and "sexual immorality" (NIV and Phillips). *Akatharsia* is usually rendered "impurity" (NJB, NRSV, NIV, and my translation) though J. B. Phillips prefers "dirty-mindedness." "Evil desires" (*epithymian kakēn*) is generally acceptable as a translation (NJB, NRSV, NIV, Phillips, and my translation); so too is "greed" (NJB, NRSV, NIV) or "insatiable greed" (my translation) for *pleonexia*, but AV/KJV translates it as "covetousness," and Phillips renders it as "lust for other people's goods," which is an accurate translation of the Greek word.

From the list of former sins Paul picks out impurity and covetousness. These were considered by Jews in Paul's day to be typical sins of the gentile world. Today we might add cruelty, in view of wars and slavery. These all represent vivid ways of self-seeking or egoism. Danker renders covetousness (*pleonexia*) as "desiring to have more than is one's due, greediness, insatiableness, avarice, covetousness."[23] Lincoln argues that "covetousness" "is the insatiable greed whereby people assume that things or other people exist

---

20. Scott, *Colossians, Philemon, and Ephesians*, 65.

21. MacDonald, *Colossians, Ephesians*, 135.

22. See Carrington, *The Primitive Christian Catechism*; and Selwyn, *First Epistle of St Peter*, Essay II.

23. Danker, BDAG, 824.

simply for their own gratification."[24] Martin writes that it is "the sin of possessiveness, an insatiable desire to lay hands on material things (cf. Luke 12:15)."[25] Moule suggests that acquisitiveness in any form is the desire to *get*, the opposite of the desire to give.[26]

Wesley expounds on Paul's association of greed and idolatry when he observes that the keen desire for what is not ours "is giving [our] heart to a creature."[27] Lohse similarly comments, "Covetousness and greed seize the heart of man, and lead it away from God, and imprison it in idolatry."[28] Covetousness is linked with idolatry because in it we have put self in the place of God. Alternatively, in Rabbinic literature "idolatry" is often specified in order to emphasize the seriousness of the sin in question. Strack and Billerbeck enumerate examples of this kind.[29] So perhaps Paul is simply stressing just *how bad* greed is when he calls it idolatry.

Wright observes, "Sin begins when the idea of illicit gratification, presented to the mind in temptation, is not at once put to death, but is instead fondled and cherished."[30] Caird adds, "If this faith is to be credible, their outward, visible conduct must conform to the realities of the new life of faith."[31] This is why Paul calls the community to "Treat as dead, therefore, your earthly limbs" (v. 5).

The words "Treat as dead" address in part the tension felt by Christians that on the one hand they are completely new, while on the other hand they are still entangled with earthly and sinful conditions. One writer suggests that Paul has two ways of dealing with this. One is to stress that Christians still wait for the redemption of our body, as in Rom 8:23; the other is to demand that their "earthly limbs" (i.e., their earthbound desires rooted in

24. Lincoln, *Colossians*, 642.

25. Martin, *Colossians and Philemon*, 104.

26. Moule, *Colossians and Philemon*, 116.

27. Wesley, *Colossians*, 27.

28. Lohse, *Colossians and Philemon*, 138.

29. Strack and Billerbeck, *Kommentar zum Neuen Testament aus Talmud und Midrasch*.

30. Wright, *Colossians and Philemon*, 139.

31. Caird, *Paul's Letters from Prison*, 203.

sin-distorted, embodied human life) are put to death, mortified.[32] But these two are not necessarily alternatives: Scott comments, "The erring Christian . . . is not living up to his true self. . . . There is a better nature in us which must not be defeated."[33]

According to v. 6, the vices are so serious that they provoke the wrath of God. The wrath of God is an important theme in Paul, except that whereas the love of God is eternal, his wrath constitutes a disposition to respond to human alienation and disobedience. It is often wrongly assumed that wrath is the opposite of love. But the opposite of love is indifference. A parent or grandparent who loves a child will not remain indifferent if the child is bent on self-destruction. Not to react would be a sign of indifference, which would not help the child. In the same way, God's wrath is often a sign of his ultimate love. In v. 6, Paul tells the readers that if the old life still holds sway, God's wrath comes upon them. Calvin writes that God's anger is set before us here that "we may be deterred from sinning."[34] Probably the phrase "the sons of disobedience" was not in the original text of Colossians but was borrowed from Eph 6:3.

Our translation "used to live" (Gk, *ezēte*) in v. 7 reflects the imperfect tense, which is past but continuous. The tense of the word contrasts with "you once walked" (Gk, *periepatēsate pote*), which is aorist (often signifying a point in time). The two types of past tense are significant. What was once a seriously bad habit has been left behind in the past. The pattern of what we "used to do" is contrasted with the present, as it was in 1 Cor 6:9–11.

Both stand in contrast to the "but now" (Gk, *nuni de*) of v. 8. Both "but now" and "you" are emphatic, but we cannot translate this as "you lay aside" for the verb is imperative ("lay aside!"), not indicative. Their former pagan attitudes or qualities are summed up as "all of them," and then enumerated separately as "anger, bad temper, malice, abusive language, obscene language from your mouth" (Gk, *orgēn, thymon, kakian, blasphēmian, aischrologian ek*

32. Scott, *Colossians, Philemon, and Ephesians*, 65–66.

33. Scott, *Colossians, Philemon, and Ephesians*, 66.

34. Calvin, *Philippians, Colossians and Thessalonians*, 209.

tou stomatos hymōn). Lincoln notes that lists of five are frequent in Colossians, and now in v. 8 Paul formulates another such list,[35] beginning with anger (Gk, *orgē*), which is evaluated negatively in Prov 15:1, 18, 22–24; Eccl 7:9; and in Hellenistic Judaism (Sir 1:22; 27:30; T. Dan 2:1—5:1). In Paul it is synonymous with "rage" (Gk, *thymos*), although Stoic writers sometimes distinguished them. Diogenes Laertius regarded rage as an explosion of anger.[36] Moulton comments, "The second list concerns sins of the mind and the mouth, sins normally regarded as trivial, except in the pure light of Christ."[37]

In vv. 8–10, Paul uses the metaphor of clothing through the use of four different words: especially for putting off, and putting on, clothes (Gk, *apothesthe*, v. 8; *apekdysamenoi*, v. 9; *endysamenoi*, v. 10; and *endysasthe*, v. 12). The idea is that of "laying aside" vices like a set of old clothes (representing sinful dispositions and practices) in order to "put on" a new set of clothes (cf. 3:8). Moule calls this radical reorientation of life a "reclothing."[38] The image of clothing for putting off vices and putting on virtues was widespread among Greek and Hellenistic Jewish writers. The metaphorical use of these verbs is at least as old as Aristophanes in Greek literature and as old as Job and Isaiah in Hebrew writings (Job 29:14; Isa 61:10). Scott points out that in many walks of life we have examples of soldiers donning a uniform, or a magistrate putting on official robes, and so on, to indicate taking on a new status and set of standards.[39]

The metaphor of "stripping of" and "putting on" clothes is especially associated with baptism in Christian thought, and Paul certainly would presuppose baptism here. It would have been

35. Col 3:5 contains the first list of five: sexual immorality, impurity, passion, evil desire, and covetousness.

36. Diogenes Laertius, 7.114; Seneca, *On Anger*, 3.36; Lincoln, *Colossians*, 643.

37. *Moulton, Colossians, Philemon, and Ephesians*, 48. The first list is a few verses earlier in 3:5.

38. Moule, *Colossians and Philemon*, 114.

39. Scott, *Colossians, Philemon, and Ephesians*, 68.

understood in the light of the metaphor of old and new clothing. There would have been no need for Paul to make this allusion explicit.

Bruce explicates the present imperative, "Do not go on lying" or "Stop lying" (v. 9), as follows: "You used to tell lies to one another as though it were the natural thing to do, don't do it any more."[40] Truth must characterize this body of believers. Lincoln comments that, for the author, "There can be no room for lies in the new community, because they poison communication and breed suspicion instead of mutual trust."[41] Calvin understands lying to indicate the more general denial of sincerity.[42]

The Greek has a participle, "while putting off the old self" or, better translated, "since you have put of the old self." NJB has "You have stripped off your old behavior with your old self." Colossians is here deploying an image Paul uses elsewhere. Thus, he speaks of stripping off the old way of life in Rom 6:6 and putting on Christ in Gal 3:27.

The next verse (v. 10) expresses the positive side: "You have *put on* a new self, which is being renewed with a view to full knowledge in accord with the image of his Creator." Our translation, "with a view to," constitutes an attempt to translate the simple Greek *eis*, "into," which governs "full knowledge" (Gk, *epignōsin*) "in accord with the image of his Creator." Paul's words "being renewed" show that renewal is a *continuous* process, not a yet accomplished fact.

"Here there does not exist gentile and Jew, circumcision and uncircumcision, uncivilized, foreigner, slave and free person" (v. 11). Rather than our simple "Here," NRSV has "In that renewal," which seeks to spell out the Greek *hopou*, "where." Robertson suggests that our translation "there does not exist" (Gk, *ouk en*) reflects a Greek idiom where *esti* "is" has been understood or presupposed.[43] "There is" (NRSV, NIV) seems weaker. NJB has, "There

40. Bruce, *Ephesians and Colossians*, 271–72.

41. Lincoln, *Colossians*, 643.

42. Calvin, *Philippians, Colossians and Thessalonians*, 210.

43. Robertson, *Word Pictures in the New Testament*, vol. 4, 503.

is no room for distinction between . . . ." Our "gentile and Jew" renders "Greek and Jew," which is explicated in the next verse as "circumcision and uncircumcision." The Greek *barbaros*, barbarian, refers to "one who is neither Greek nor Roman" (i.e., someone who is, in Roman opinion, uncivilized), while Scythian (*Skythēs*) is an example of a very remote "barbarian." Thus, Scythian likely indicates "the distant foreigner." Caird suggests that both "barbarian" and "Scythian" were pejorative terms used by Greeks.[44] Every first-century reader would understand the contrast between slave and free.

Loyalty to Christ takes precedence over all divisive ties. NJB has, "There is only Christ: he is everything and in everything," which well sums up Paul's concern. Such equality in Christ was earlier affirmed in Gal 3:28 and 1 Cor 12:13—where there is neither male nor female, Jew and gentile, and slave and free person in Christ—and remains prominent for him even in this later epistle. Paul is emphasizing equality more strongly than modern Western societies might appreciate; in their original context, where status and value were dependent on one social identity, his words would resonate as radically egalitarian.

Questions for reflection

1. How can we cultivate a mind that is so absorbed with Christ that we cease to be preoccupied with the pull of our Christless self?

2. What does Paul mean by "above"? Does it mean "higher up," or where Christ is "seated" with honor and authority? What does Christ being "seated" imply?

3. Why must we "keep on thinking" of Christ in his realm? What happens if we do not do this? Why should our "death" from the "old" everyday existence matter?

44. Caird, *Paul's Letters from Prison*, 206.

4. What hints are given of the future that Christians, who are raised with Christ, can expect?

5. Why does Paul's list of vices often correspond in different passages? Is it surprising that Christians are often accused of placing too much emphasis on sexual vices?

6. How does longing for what does not belong to us lead to idolatry? Why does this provoke God to anger? Has someone's anger ever helped us? What does "the wrath of God" really mean? How does it differ from his love?

7. Why does Paul so often use the metaphor of changing clothes to illustrate the radical transformation of the self?

8. How important are sins of speech in vv. 8 and 9? Does this emphasis balance that on sexual sins earlier?

9. Is the image of God something that we were born with, or a goal into which we seek to be transformed?

10. Is anger always a bad thing? What about our reaction to injustice? Or has the pendulum swung too far today?

2. The distinctive character of the Christian (3:12–17)

12 As chosen, holy, and beloved people of God, then, put on a heart of compassion, kindness, humility, meekness, and patience, **13** forbearing one another and forgiving each other if anyone has a complaint against anyone, even as the Lord forgave you, so you also must forgive. **14** On top of all these clothes, put on love, which is the perfect bond. **15** And may the peace of Christ rule in your hearts for which purpose you were called in one body; and keep being thankful. **16** Let the word of Christ dwell in you richly, teaching and admonishing one another in all wisdom, and with thanksgiving sing psalms, hymns, and spiritual songs in your hearts to God. **17** Whatever you may do in word or deed, do everything

in the name of the Lord Jesus, giving thanks to God the
Father through him.[45]

As Martin urges, the readers may have thought that Paul was being
impossibly idealistic, so in vv. 12–17 he now seeks to offer specific,
practical, and detailed guidance about the conduct that the new
life demands.[46] Martin continues: Paul gives (i) a list of virtues to
be cultivated (v. 12); (ii) a statement about how Christians are to
react if they become disturbed (v. 13); and (iii) the principle that
love is the distinctive badge of the Christian life (v. 14). (iv) Christ's
peace will act as arbiter when choices have to be made (v. 15). And
(v) the church's worship will both promote praise to God (v. 16)
and bring everything under the spirit of devotion to Jesus Christ
(v. 17).

Paul addresses those who are God's chosen people on whom
God has placed his love. These were qualities of Israel in the Old
Testament, and this establishes that the Christ-community is in-
corporated through Israel's Messiah, Jesus, into the election of the
chosen nation.

Lincoln comments, "The five virtues listed in 3:12 are those
required for harmonious living in a community."[47] The believers
are "to put on" (like new clothes) a compassionate heart, kindness,
humility, meekness, and patience. Moule describes "meekness"
(Gk, *prautēs*) as "willingness to make concessions."[48] He adds
that these qualities may be called "ordinary" virtues. "Meekness" becomes clear when we set it in contrast with its opposite,
"rudeness." "Patience" means "long-temperedness" and refers to

---

45. Textual notes: In v. 13 the UBS Committee found it difficult to decide
about the Gk, *kyrios,* the Lord. The case is finely balanced, but "the Lord" may
be accepted. In v. 14 some MSS (D*, F, G) read Gk, *henotētos,* "which holds
them together," rather than Gk, *teleiotētos,* "perfect" (Sinaiticus, A, B, and C).
In v. 16 "word of Christ" may be accepted (with Þ46, Sinaiticus C, B and D),
although usually the phrase is "word of God" (here A, C*, and 33). In v. 17 "to
God the Father" is almost certain and is supported by the earliest MSS.

46. Martin, *Colossians and Philemon,* 109.

47. Lincoln, *Colossians,* 647.

48. Moule, *Colossians and Philemon,* 123.

endurance in the face of wrong or exasperating conduct. Its opposite is flying into a rage.

Paul does not imagine that Christians never do anything wrong; rather, they know how to deal with faults and complaints by mutual forbearance and forgiveness (v. 13). Christians are to curb their impatience in difficult situations. It is characteristic of Paul to recall the self-sacrifice of Christ in his account of salvation to provide the motive for Christians to turn their bitterness into forgiving love.

"On top of these" (v. 14) probably refers to an outer garment that can cover all the other clothes, which would reinforce the metaphor of changing into new clothes. In other words, on top of all these virtues with which you are now dressed put on the outer garment of love. On the other hand, it could simply mean "above all" in the elative sense ("elative" means the superlative degree).[49] In other words, put on these virtues, and most especially love. Lincoln warns us that it is not clear how far the image of clothing can be extended, but most writers take the former view and see the writer as making a probable reference to outer clothing.[50] "The perfect bond" denotes what binds everything together in perfect harmony. Love can bind all together, completing the whole. As we noted, some MSS read "united" or "in harmony" in place of "perfect." Paul also expounded the centrality of love elsewhere (1 Corinthians 13; Rom 13:8, 10; and Gal 5:6).

"The peace of Christ" that is to rule in their hearts (v. 15) refers to the peace between people that Christ brings. Paul stresses the need for a Christian community to live together in unity and tolerance. Wright comments, "The *pax Christiana* is to prevail in the church, as the *pax Romana* did in the world of Paul's day."[51] Where there might be conflict, the umpire is the peace that Christ brings. "Rule" (Gk, *brabeuein*) also means "to arbitrate," as in a legal case or athletic contest. Martin writes, "The harmony of the

---

49. Moule, *Colossians and Philemon*, 123.

50. Lincoln, *Colossians*, 648.

51. Wright, *Colossians and Philemon*, 148.

Church is God's will for his people."[52] In a similar way, in Eph 2:14 "Christ is our peace" refers to the relational unity established in Christ between Jews and gentiles. A new society of "wholeness" comes into being. "Heart"—where the peace of Christ is to rule—has varied meanings in the Old Testament. It could be the seat of deep feeling, including fear and joy (1 Sam 2:1), or the sphere of reflection or comfort, but it is also the center or core of a person, which may become hard or obstinate. Jewett calls it "the center of . . . will and emotion."[53] Nevertheless, in spite of this emphasis on the hearts of individuals in the church, we must not envisage this peace in individualist ways (i.e., as inner calm); rather, the peace in their hearts necessarily flows inter-relationally between members of the community. The peace in question *is* peace between persons. McKnight observes that, "Peace is at the heart of ethics for Paul in Colossians."[54]

The earliest Christian communities made much of singing praises to God. Yet, as Moule observes on vv. 16–17, "The vocal praise is to be accompanied by an inward spirit of praise."[55] Everything done and said by community members must be done and said in Jesus' name, and motivated by hearts thankful towards God.

Questions for reflection

1. Why does Paul seem almost to labor the metaphor of setting aside one set of clothes and putting on another? How helpful do you find that metaphor?

2. What qualities ascribed to Israel are now said to also characterize the Christ-community?

52. Martin, *Colossians and Philemon*, 113.

53. Jewett, *Paul's Anthropological Terms*, 144; and Behm, "*Kardia* in the New Testament," 611.

54. McKnight, *Colossians*, 326.

55. Moule, *Colossians and Philemon*, 126.

3. What "ordinary, everyday" virtues are expected of the Christian? Why does Paul use "lists" of virtues?

4. How do these virtues defuse contentions and complaints against us from fellow Christians? How do we react to others who might criticize us?

5. In what sense can love be like an outer garment that covers and binds together all the other virtues?

6. How can Christ's peace become an arbiter or umpire? What happens if our hearts are not dominated by Christ's peace?

7. What are the effects of letting the word of Christ dwell richly in us? What does this achieve in addition to "wisdom" and "teaching"?

8. Do we sing hymns, psalms, and inspired songs with thanksgiving, or do we sing in church simply out of duty?

9. In what sense can we do everything we say or do in the name of the Lord Jesus Christ?

10. Are our prayers normally directed to God the Father, through our Lord Jesus Christ?

3. Life within the household as it is affected by Christianity (3:18—4:1)

18 You wives, be in subjection to your husbands as is fitting in the Lord. 19 You husbands, keep on loving your wives and stop being harsh with them. 20 As for you children, obey your parents in everything, for this is well pleasing in the Lord. 21 You fathers, do not irritate your children lest they become discouraged. 22 You slaves, be obedient in every way to those who are your earthly masters, not only when you are under their eye as those seeking to win their favor, but in singleness of heart, and reverence for the Lord. 23 Whatever you do, work at it wholeheartedly, working as to the Lord and not to human people, 24 knowing that from the Lord you will

receive an inheritance as your reward; you serve the Lord
Christ. **25** Anyone who does wrong will be paid back for
whatever wrong has been done; and there is no partiality. **4:1** You masters, make provision for your slaves to be
given what is right and fair, knowing that you also have a
master in heaven.[56]

Lohse and some others suggest that Paul introduces an indepen-
dent and "self-contained" series of admonitions about "household
rules" in v. 18.[57] He proposes Hellenistic and Jewish parallels, as
well as others in the New Testament. Moule, on the other hand, argues that, on the assumption that Colossians is earlier than Ephesians and 1 Peter, this is probably the earliest example of the ethics
of the household in the New Testament. (New Testament parallels
are found in Eph 5:22—6:9; 1 Tim 2:8–15; Titus 2:1–10; and 1 Pet
2:13—3:7.) Although there are similar examples in Epictetus, Diogenes Laertius, and other secular writers, in Christian households
"the stress [is] upon the *reciprocal* nature of the duties."[58] Indeed,
Eph 5:21 enjoins *mutual* submission.

Lincoln discusses the wider currency of "household rules" in
the Greco-Roman world of the time, from which Philo and the
Jewish synagogue derived them. They were drawn ultimately from
the classical Greek philosophers and continued until the later Roman period. Proper household management was a primary concern. In their commentaries, Lincoln and Lohse both devote an
excursus to "the Household Code,"[59] and both emphasize that
the Christian instinct was not to flee from the everyday life of the
world, but to engage in routine domestic duties. Christians, they
note, did not seek to destabilize society. (Epictetus and Diogenes
Laertius similarly commended ethical attitudes that related to a

56. Textual note: in v. 21 "do not irritate" (Gk, *mē erethizete*) or provoke
or excite into an unstable state of mind is graded "almost certain" by the UBS
Committee, supported by Þ46 Sinaiticus and B. Later readings adopt Gk,
parorgizete, to provoke to anger, from Eph 6:4 (Metzger, *A Textual Commentary on the New Testament*, 558).

57. Lohse, *Colossians and Philemon*, 154; cf. 155–57.

58. Moule, *Colossians and Philemon*, 127. Italics mine.

59. Lincoln, *Colossians*, 652–54; Lohse, *Colossians and Philemon*, 154–57.

person's immediate situation.) The false teachers in Colossae urged the very opposite, with visionary experiences, magic, and asceticism. They were too preoccupied with supposed "heavenly things" and heavenly beings to leave much room for everyday concerns about the home and family. Perhaps the early use of "Household Rules" reflect a response to pagan criticisms that Christian faith sought to undermine society. In Colossians, the context of the Household Code is that of wisdom, behaving wisely, and being centered on Christ.

Scott comments, "Christianity has in no way effected a deeper change in the world's life than by placing the family on a new basis. The family is the fundamental social unit and the remodeling of it meant nothing less than the reconstruction of human society in its whole extent."[60] He admits that this was in no small degree an inheritance from Judaism, but Christianity became the means by which this Jewish approach to family was diffused more widely.

The addition of "you" in "You wives" simply reflects the regular use of the definite article to indicate a vocative (lit. "The wives"). Lohse points out that in the LXX the Semitic vocative is rendered in this way.[61] Robertson argues that "you wives" best renders the Greek, but no main English version (except Goodspeed) follows this (including NJB, NRSV, NIV, and AV/KJB).[62] "Be in subjection" (Gk, *hypotassesthe*) is a military metaphor that stresses order. Wives have rights and privileges, but the home is to be well ordered. Else Kähler argues that this verb indicates entirely *voluntary* subjection for the sake of order.[63] Wright comments, "Paul offers a careful balance. Neither party is to be arrogant or domineering."[64] Caird points out that some Christian wives would be married to unbelieving husbands, and some Christian husbands would be married to unbelieving wives.[65]

60. Scott, *Colossians, Philemon, and Ephesians*, 77.

61. Lohse, *Colossians and Philemon*, 157, n.16.

62. Robertson, *Word Pictures in the New Testament*, vol. 4, 506.

63. Kähler, *Die Frau in den paulinischen Briefen*, 156.

64. Wright, *Colossians and Philemon*, 152.

65. Caird, *Paul's Letters from Prison*, 208.

Husband are to "keep on loving" (v. 19). The phrase renders the present active imperative, and Harris has "make it your practice to love." The second command to husbands in relation to their wives—"Do not make bitter" or "do not become embittered" (Gk, *mē pikrainesthe*)—is also a present middle imperative. RSV, NEB, GNB, and NIV have "do not be harsh with them."

There is such widespread talk about equal rights today that many will find the injunctions in 3:18 shocking. It certainly comes from a cultural context very different from our own and we need to try to understand it within its world. In his International Critical Commentary, Wilson writes that this verse "does not necessarily mean that women were mere chattels submissively enduring a life little better than slaves at the mercy of their husbands."[66] He stresses that this verse does not refer to women in general, including single women and widows, but only to wives. He points out that women such as Phoebe and Chloe were heads of houses, who could perform leadership roles or run businesses. McKnight points out that women married at an age earlier than is the custom in our world, namely twelve to thirteen years old in the Roman world, and a little later in the Jewish world. He and most other commentators also point out that the relationship with husbands carries reciprocal responsibilities, as is amplified in Ephesians in greater detail (Eph 5:22–33). Husbands are told to love their wives *as their own bodies.*[67] Similarly, in Ephesians, Paul urges Christians to submit *to one another* (Eph 5:21), indicating that there was a mutuality in submission and it was not one-way traffic. Colossians offers only a very reduced summary of this fuller teaching. Paul anchors his instructions to wives by "as is fitting in the Lord." McKnight argues that "in the Lord" "dramatically changes the entire expression and makes any connection to Stoicism at best remote."[68] He says that "fitting" means Christoformity (i.e., being formed in Christlike ways). He further adds, "Superiority, power, and status have all

---

66. Wilson, *Colossians and Philemon*, 276.

67. McKnight, *Colossians*, 342–43.

68. McKnight, *Colossians*, 344, n.229.

been eradicated in Christoformity."[69] So Paul takes conventional understandings of husband-wife relationships and then plants in them Christian ingredients that radically transform and reshape those relationships from within.

Lincoln comments on v. 20: "The advice to children and parents is included because it is one of the three basic relationships treated in the discussion of household management in the Aristotelian tradition. . . . Attacks on the Christian movement also spoke of their subversion of children."[70] Children should obey their parents. "Obey" in v. 20 is parallel to "be subject to" in v. 18. Paul adds that children are to obey their parents "in all respects" (BADG) or "at every point" (Moffatt) rather than "in everything" (NERB, Weymouth). Such obedience is "well pleasing in the Lord." The phrase "in the Lord" may mean "among Christians" or "as befits those who belong to the Lord" (Harris). Lightfoot takes the Greek, *euareston* (well pleasing) in a secular sense as "commendable."[71] But normally in biblical usage the word means "pleasing *to God.*"

The guidance is not one-way. "Fathers," Lincoln observes, "have obligations, as do their children."[72] Fathers are instructed not to provoke children. The Greek *mē erethizete* means do not provoke, irritate, exasperate or excite. Moffatt has "avoid irritating," while NEB and NASB have "do not exasperate." Why? The phrase *hina mē athymōsin* means "lest they be discouraged, be despondent, lose heart, or lack spirit." Scott comments, "Paul assumes that firm discipline is necessary."[73] That is so, but his point here is that such discipline needs to be tempered lest it does the children more harm than good.

The final relationship dealt with in the Household Code is that between slaves and masters (3:22—4:1). O'Brien comments, "Slaves who have become believers are to accept their station as

69. McKnight, *Colossians*, 344.

70. Lincoln, *Colossians*, 655.

71. Lightfoot, *Colossians and Philemon*, 227.

72. Lincoln, *Colossians*, 656.

73. Scott, *Colossians, Philemon, Ephesians*, 79.

slaves and to obey their earthly masters in everything."[74] "Earthly" is a normal rendering of the Greek *kata sarka* (lit. according to flesh), as in NEB, NIV, NRSV, although NJB, GNB, have "human." Presumably this is to stress that believing slaves are not simply obligated to their new heavenly master but also to their earthly masters. Paul coins the Greek word *ophthalmodoulia*, "eye-service" (which does not occur earlier than Paul), although "when you are under their eye" (NJB) admirably conveys the sense. Lohse comments, "He [Paul] calls eyeservice that type of service which does not issue from a sincere heart but is content in mere external appearance."[75] Paul also probably coins the word *anthrōpareskoi*, "people pleasers" or "men pleasers," although this does occur in Ps 52:6 (LXX) as well as Eph 6:6. The motivation of the slaves in their work must not be people-pleasing but God-pleasing. Moule contrasts work motivated by the fear of God with superficial work, "not dusting behind the ornaments, not sweeping under the wardrobe."[76] In contrast to these ambivalent motives, Paul pleads for "singleness of heart" in their obedience and reverence to the Lord. MacDonald observes that the fact that slaves are addressed directly rather than via their masters gives firm evidence that they were part of the Christian community.[77]

Christians are to serve conscientiously out of pure motives. Reverence for the Lord (Gk, *phoboumenoi ton kyrion*) refers, O'Brien argues, to *Christ* as Lord, although the same phrase in the Old Testament referred to God.[78] The verb denotes fear, awe, and reverence.

The exhortations are gathered up into a comprehensive command, "Whatever you do, work at it wholeheartedly, working as to the Lord" (v. 23). "Heartily" represents the Greek *ek psychē* (lit. out of soul/self/inner life), but "wholeheartedly" picks up Greek *en haplotēti kardias* (singleness of heart) from the previous verse. For

74. O'Brien, *Colossians, Philemon*, 226.

75. Lohse, *Colossians and Philemon*, 160.

76. Moule, *Colossians and Philemon*, 130.

77. MacDonald, *Colossians, Ephesians*, 156.

78. O'Brien, *Colossians, Philemon*, 227.

Christians service is always to the Lord, even when it appears to be offered to human people in the first place. Dunn comments, "This simply repeats what has just been said. The implication is that one of the chief dangers of the slave status was a lack of personal motivation which made all work a drudgery provided grudgingly, with lack of effort and always with a view to doing as little as one could get away with. Such an attitude can be sustained only at tremendous personal cost, with other aspects of the personality 'switched off,' withdrawn, or suppressed, or with a calculating motivation fed by resentment and bitterness."[79] The danger was such that it required repeated warning.

Rengstorf discusses the attitude to slavery in Paul more broadly in his article in Kittel.[80] The instructions on slavery are "wholly within the framework of the time and cannot be isolated from it." The word "slave" conveys a picture of bondage and limitation, but slaves are never spoken of contemptuously or disparagingly by Paul. The slave is never despised. In terms of true status, the redemptive work of Christ is decisive: in Christ there is neither slave nor free. But the concrete conditions of society still remain. The primary goal of the Christian slave "is not the attainment of freedom; it is that as a slave he should live unto the Lord like all those for whom He died."[81] This is confirmed from 1 Cor 7:17–24, and the work of David Horrell, Scott Bartchy, John Barclay, Dale Martin, Bruce Winter, and others.[82] NJB renders 1 Cor 7:21, "Even if you have the chance of freedom you should prefer to make use of your condition as a slave."[83]

In v. 24, the "reward" that good Christian slaves will receive is described as "the inheritance," perhaps alluding to the Old Testament texts concerning Israel's entry into the promised land, its

79. Dunn, *Colossians and Philemon*, 255.

80. Rengstorf, "*Doulos,* slave."

81. Rengstorf, "*Doulos,* slave," 272.

82. Cf. Thiselton, *First Epistle to the Corinthians*, 550–65 for a discussion of the modern literature.

83. On 1 Cor 7:21–22, see Bartchy, *mallon chrēsai*; Dale B. Martin, *Slavery as Salvation*, especially 63–68.

inheritance. The Greek *klēronomos* may simply mean "inherited property," as from a father to a son. If "inheritance" alludes to dwelling in the promised land, this may be equivalent to possession of the kingdom of God, i.e., in the presence of God.

"So when Paul says (v. 25) that 'the dishonest person will receive the dishonesty that he has committed,' the meaning is that dishonesty brings its own nemesis—exclusion from opposition which is possible only for one who is honest with God."[84] Paul reinforces his core point: slaves are in reality serving the Lord Christ. The phrase "the Lord Christ" is much more rare than we might imagine. It occurs only here and in Rom 16:18. Moule suggests that Paul is contrasting Christ as Lord with other lords. He also suggests that "Christ" has all but become a name rather than a title (the Anointed One, the Messiah) at this point.[85]

"Knowing," as O'Brien observes, "suggests that the apostle is recalling a pattern of teaching known to Christians: it is from the heavenly Lord that they will receive the inheritance of their reward."[86] "Reward" is used here with its positive connotations. Under Roman law a slave might not be able to inherit anything, but Christian slaves may inherit the reward from their heavenly Lord.

Slaves need to recall that God is impartial in his judgment, treating slaves and masters the same. If they do wrong then they will be paid back by God for it. The word "partiality" (Gk, *prosōpolēmpsia*) does not appear prior to New Testament times. The word reflects the Hebrew idiom for "to show partiality," which is, in the ancient idiom, "to accept the face" (LXX, Gk, *prosopon lambanein*, Lev 19:15; Job 42:8).

What of masters? Do they have obligations to slaves? Indeed, they are to treat them *right* and *fair* (*to dikaion kai tēn isotēta*) in the knowledge that *they themselves* are slaves in service of a heavenly Master (4:1). The phrase "right and fair" has to do with equity, not equality. Before Christ as their Master both slaves and free persons

---

84. Moule, *Colossians and Philemon*, 131.

85. Moule, *Colossians and Philemon*, 131.

86. O'Brien, *Colossians, Philemon*, 228.

stand *on the same footing*.[87] God shows no partiality. Righteous behavior is required of master and slaves alike. In a similar vein, in 2 Cor 5:10 Paul had written, "For we must *all* appear before the judgement seat of Christ that each one may receive what is due to him for the things done while in the body, whether good or bad."

Questions for reflection

1. Are we concerned by Paul's injunctions in the light of changing attitudes towards women? What does "being in subjection" entail? Does it mean more than an ordered life? Might marriages fail because someone wants to dominate?

2. How vital is it to stop bitterness from spoiling family relationships? What causes bitterness? What is responsible behavior?

3. Are these three sets of relationships all about power or about something else? What reciprocal obligations are placed upon fathers and husbands? Might marriages fail if they degenerate into a struggle for power?

4. What does how we live in the home and family say about our faith? Is Christian witness tested in everyday life or in times of crisis? Do principles about "slaves and masters" apply to employers and employees?

5. If the whole family lives under the Lordship of Christ, what does this imply about the place of anger, rage, abusive language, conflict, and peace? What changes are suggested if only a part of the family is Christian?

6. Is Jesus Christ's submission to God the Father a pattern for us all to follow? How much did Jesus listen to his Father in order to live in subjection to his purpose?

7. Does constant criticism and reprimand destroy a child's sense of worth? How can discipline be balanced and consistent? What is the value of small acts of kindness?

87. Caird, *Paul's Letters from Prison*, 209.

8. How can values from the first century be carried over into modern democratic society?

9. Can we avoid the temptation to get by with as little work as possible? How can we learn to put our whole heart into our work as an offering to God in Christ our Lord?

4. Final Instructions: prayer, mission, and contact with outsiders (4:2-6)

> **2** Be busily engaged in prayer, keeping alert while at prayer with an attitude of thanksgiving. **3** Pray at the same time for us also that God may open to us a door for his word to proclaim the mystery of Christ, for which I am also a prisoner. **4** This is in order that I may make it known as I ought to proclaim it. **5** Walk wisely in the face of those who are outside, redeeming the moment of opportunity. **6** Let your speech always be gracious, seasoned with salt, and be sensitive to the kind of answer each one requires.[88]

"Be busily engaged in" prayer (v. 2) translates Greek *proskartereite*, which Danker renders "to busy oneself with, be busily engaged in, be devoted to," alongside "persevere in," and "continue in."[89] This fits evidence in Acts and Romans as well as in contemporary papyri. Wright has "devote yourselves to prayer" and Robertson has "continue steadfastly in prayer."[90] The Greek *grēgorountes en autē* means they are to engage in it (i.e., prayer) while keeping awake, being watchful, alert, or vigilant; we have substituted "while at prayer" for "in it" to explicate the pronoun "it." Moffatt translates, "Maintain your zest for prayer." Lightfoot argues that since long continuance in prayer is apt to produce listlessness, Paul gives

---

88. Textual note: In v. 3 in place of "the mystery of Christ" a few witnesses (B*, L) read "mystery of God."

89. Danker, BDAG, 881.

90. Robertson, *Word Pictures in the New Testament*, vol. 4, 509.

the additional charge that the heart must be awake.[91] Caird comments, "Prayer is a watchful readiness for opportunities."[92] Prayer and thanksgiving "should be the pervading mood of the Christian life."[93] Lincoln writes, "A life characterized by prayer is a recognition of our creaturely dependence on God."[94]

Paul asks that the Colossians remember to pray for him and his co-workers that they may have opportunities—expressed by means of the metaphor of a door opening—to proclaim Christ (v. 3).[95] Robertson comments, "It is comforting to other preachers to see the greatest of all preachers here asking prayer that he may be set free again to preach. He uses this figure elsewhere, once of a great and open door with many adversaries in Ephesus (1 Cor. 16:29), once of an open door that he could not enter in Troas (2 Cor. 2:12)."[96] The letter began with Paul's assurance that he prayed for the Colossians; the final part of the letter asks them to pray for him. As Dunn observes, this underlines the indispensability of prayer for Paul and the early Pauline mission.[97] Calvin writes, "Who, then, in this present day, would dare to despise the intercessions of brethren, which Paul openly declares himself to stand in need of?"[98]

Paul had a gospel fire in his bones and wanted to preach, even during his captivity (v. 3), as he implies in Phil 1:12–14: "I want you to know . . . that what has happened to me has actually helped to spread the gospel, so that it has become known throughout the whole Imperial Guard and to everyone else that my imprisonment

---

91. Lightfoot, *Colossians and Philemon*, 231.

92. Caird, *Paul's Letters from Prison*, 209.

93. Scott, *Colossians, Philemon and Ephesians*, 83.

94. Lincoln, *Colossians*, 663.

95. When Paul asks the Colossians to "pray . . . for *us* also," Macdonald comments that "us" could refer only to Paul, but more probably it refers to the evangelistic efforts he shares with co-workers such as Timothy (1:1) and Epaphras (4:12–13) (MacDonald, *Colossians, Ephesians*, 171).

96. Robertson, *Word Pictures in the new Testament*, vol. 4, 509.

97. Dunn, *Colossians and Philemon*, 262.

98. Calvin, *Philippians, Colossians, and Thessalonians*, 223.

is for Christ." But he also expresses the hope that the gospel will spread throughout the whole world (1:5–6).

Although Paul is using the word "speak" in vv. 3 and 4, Mac-Donald and Dunn propose "proclaim" is a more suitable translation in this context. This includes prayer for speaking with clarity and conviction concerning what was once hidden but is now revealed in the gospel. Does this imply that in spite of his wonderful preaching, Paul was "never satisfied with it" (Robertson)? What preacher, Robertson asks, can be? Paul has a clear sense of how he "ought" (Gk, *dei*, v. 4) to proclaim the gospel. Dunn observes that this "ought" expresses "Paul's burning conviction and sense of destiny which no doubt sustained Paul through a ministry of astonishing exertion and suffering [and] made it so effective."[99]

"Walk wisely in the face of those who are outside, redeeming the moment of opportunity" (v. 5). Caird writes, "Christians are to have a sense of urgency, but it must not make them insensitive to public opinion: outsiders are not to be needlessly offended or antagonised by untimely criticisms of their way of life."[100] Bruce comments that in Paul's day distorted accounts of Christian behavior and belief were in circulation; it was thus especially important that Christians should give no color to these calumnies, but should rather give the lie to them by their ordinary manner of life.[101] Many who are not Christians, he adds, may not read the Bible or listen to the preaching of the word of God; but they can see the lives of those who do, and form their judgement accordingly. Let Christians make full use of this present time on earth of opportunity.

Here the exhortation to "redeem the time" (v. 5, repeated in Eph 5:16) seems to have special application to their duty to unbelieving neighbors. It also implies that every moment is precious. Paul has addressed the issue of how Christians must behave in the home; now it addresses how they must behave in the world.

---

99. Dunn, *Colossians and Philemon*, 264.

100. Caird, *Paul's Letters from Prison*, 210.

101. Bruce, *Ephesians and Colossians*, 299.

Wright comments, "Blameless life lays the foundation for gracious witness, as Christians make the most of every opportunity."[102]

Well-seasoned words are what is called for. Seasoned with salt was a familiar idiom in the first century. Scott observes, "In ordinary Greek this metaphor was often used for sparkling conversation."[103] Plutarch uses the metaphor of salt for speech, especially for witty speech. He says, "For wit is probably the tastiest condiment of all. Therefore some call it graciousness because it makes the necessary chore of eating pleasant."[104] Salt also occurs in the teaching of Jesus (Matt 5:13; Mark 9:49–50; Luke 14:34–35). NJB has: "Always talk pleasantly and with a flavor of wit." Dunn states that this excludes the notion of the church as a "holy huddle," which speaks only "the language of Zion" to insiders . . . , but is engaged in regular conversation with others."[105] He adds that this picture is as far as we can imagine from that of the Christian who has no interest in affairs outside those of faith or church and no "small talk." "Such conversations, however, regularly and quite naturally—throw up opportunities to bear more specific Christian witness—not as something artificially added on to a "secular" conversation, nor requiring special language or manner of speaking, but as part of a typical exchange of opinions and ideas."[106]

Questions for reflection

1. Do we keep alert while persevering in prayer or do we too easily become distracted?

2. Are our prayers shot through with thanksgiving?

3. How much do we pray for pastors and preachers? Do we pray for their further opportunities for the gospel?

102. Wright, *Colossians and Philemon*, 157.
103. Scott, *Colossians, Philemon, and Ephesians*, 85.
104. Plutarch, *Moralia* 514EF and 685A; cited in Danker, BDAG, 41.
105. Dunn, *Colossians and Philemon*, 266.
106. Dunn, *Colossians and Philemon*, 267.

4. Do we sufficiently recognize how often pastors and preachers long to do better?

5. How often do we pray for those in prison or some kind of restriction?

6. Are we concerned to live wisely and blamelessly in public before those who are not Christians?

7. Do we limit our contact with outsiders by living in "a holy huddle" or do we have social intercourse with those outside our church?

8. How gracious is our conversation with others?

9. Do we view time as precious and seek to make use of every opportunity?

10. Are we sensitive or gruff with those whom we seek to influence for Christ?

IV

Personal Notes

Paul's Messengers and His Companions, and Final Greetings

4:7–18

7 Tychicus will tell you about all my affairs. He is my beloved brother and faithful minister and fellow servant in the Lord. 8 I am sending him to you precisely for this very purpose: that you may know how we are and may find heartfelt encouragement. 9 With him I am sending Onesimus, my faithful and beloved brother, who is from your community. They will let you know everything that is happening here. 10 Aristarchus, my fellow prisoner, greets you, and Mark, the cousin of Barnabas, concerning whom you have received instructions. If he comes to you, welcome him. 11 Jesus, who is surnamed Justus adds his greetings. These are the only Jewish converts among my co-workers for the kingdom of God, and they have proved a comfort to me. 12 Epaphras, slave of Christ, who is from your community, greets you. He is always wrestling in prayer on your behalf that with maturity and conviction you may stand firm in doing the

will of God. **13** I testify for him that he works tirelessly on your behalf and on behalf of those in Laodicea and those in Hierapolis. **14** Luke, the dearly loved doctor, sends you his greetings; and so does Demas. **15** Give my greetings to the brothers and sisters in Laodicea, and to Nympha and the church in her house. **16** When this letter has been read aloud at your gathering, have it read in the church of Laodicea; and see that you in turn read the letter from Laodicea. **17** And tell Archippus: "Attend to the Christian ministry that you have received in the Lord, so that you may discharge it fully." **18** This greeting comes from Paul—in my own hand. Remember my chains. Grace be with you.[1]

Tychicus, whose name means "Mr. Fortunate,"[2] was a trusted co-worker of Paul, a "fellow servant" (just as Epaphras is described in 1:7). Paul describes him as "faithful," which has the sense of "reliable."[3] He was the bearer of the letter to the Ephesians (Eph 6:21–22) as well as this letter to the Colossians (v. 7). Tychicus was a native of the province of Asia (Acts 20:4), perhaps Ephesus. Maybe that is why Paul sent him on a mission to Ephesus, according to 2 Tim 4:12. Tychicus also accompanied Paul on the important mission of carrying the collection of the gentile churches to the poor in Jerusalem. He it is who will give the Colossians all the news (*ta kat' eme* means "my circumstances") about Paul (v. 7). Verses 7–8 are virtually identical to Eph 6:21–22. Moulton

1. Textual notes: In v. 8 "that you may know how we are" is almost certain, and is supported by A, B, D*, 33, Coptic (Sahidic) and most Syriac MSS. Þ46 and the corrector of Sinaiticus produced nonsense by substituting "how you are" for "how we are." Some MSS tried to clear up the confusion (Cf. Metzger, *A Textual Commentary on the New Testament*, 559–60). In v. 12 The UBS Committee had difficulty in deciding whether to read "slave of Christ" or "slave of Christ Jesus." In v. 15 the gender of Nympha is uncertain. Similarly MSS vary on "his" and "her." The UBS Committee favored the feminine, partly it was supported by B and other MSS.

2. Moulton, *Colossians, Philemon and Ephesians*, 65.

3. O'Brien, *Colossians, Philemon*, 247.

suggests that Tychicus was asked to fill in personal details on each occasion.[4]

The Greek past tense of *pempō* (to send) in v. 8 (lit. "I sent") is to be understood as an "epistolary aorist" (Gk, *epempsa*) with a present meaning. It is past only from the retrospective perspective of the readers. At the time of writing Paul has obviously not yet sent Tychicus with the letter. Thus, we translate it "I am sending him." Paul is sending him so that the Colossians may know how Paul's team are doing. "That you may know" (Gk, *hina gnōte*) is technically an "ingressive" aorist,[5] meaning "that you may come to know." The Greek idiom *eis auto* means literally "for this itself" and can be conveyed by "for this very purpose" or "for this very reason." "Tychicus was a particularly valued colleague"[6] and he can convey Paul's presence to the Colossians more than Paul can express by mere writing. "Know how we are" (Gk, *ta peri hēmōn*) is rendered "our circumstances" by TCNT, NASB, and NIV.

Onesimus is the co-bearer of the letter with Tychicus (v. 9). He is praised by Paul equally, even though he is a runaway slave, about whom Paul writes in Philemon. Because of his conversion he is no longer alone but is a trustworthy member of the community and the apostolic band. He can now accept a responsible task. Dunn comments, "He must be given a fanfare similar to that for Tychicus: 'faithful and beloved brother.'"[7] We translate "from your community" because the Greek "from you" does not specify whether "you" refers to the city (political identity) or the church (Christian identity). Probably both are understood, but now after his conversion the church is primary.

Now in v. 10 greetings come from the trio of those who are said to be the only Jewish Christian co-workers of Paul and who are commended as having been a comfort to him. Aristarchus was from Thessalonica and accompanied Paul to Jerusalem with the

4. Moulton, *Colossians, Philemon and Ephesians*, 65.

5. "Ingressive" means denoting entrance upon a state; "aorist" denotes a past action conceived as a whole.

6. O'Brien, *Colossians, Philemon*, 247.

7. Dunn, *Colossians and Philemon*, 273.

collection from the gentile churches (Acts 19:29; 20:4). He is now in Rome with Paul. The Greek *synaichmalōtos mou* may have been coined by Paul, and probably means "fellow prisoner" or more properly, "fellow prisoner of war" (Caird and Moule), although it may refer to his Christian service.[8] Abbott argues for literal imprisonment, but Moule argues otherwise.[9]

The New Testament gives more information about Mark, the second of the three (v. 10). Paul had once separated from him (Acts 15:36–39), but now cordially commended him. Mark's rift with Paul was clearly temporary. The Colossians, says Paul, are to offer Mark a hospitable reception if he comes to them. As an aside, Moule points that two of the men traditionally considered to be Gospel writers, Mark (v. 10) and Luke (v. 14), were mentioned here as being with Paul.[10] Mark is the "cousin" (Gk, *anepsios*) of Barnabas. (*Anepsios* meant "nephew" in very late Greek but meant "cousin" in Paul's day and in papyri.) Paul refers to Barnabas here as if he were well known in Colossae.[11]

Jesus is the third member of the trio (v. 11). The name "Jesus" occurs frequently, meaning "Joshua." The surname "Justus" represents the Greek *dikaios*, like the Hebrew Zadok. Jesus Justus is unknown to us except in this reference. Paul designates the trio as being of "the circumcision," which simply means that they were Jewish. Mark, Aristarchus, and Jesus Justus then were the three Jewish Christ-believers who accompanied Paul. Luke and Epaphras, by contrast, were gentile Christians. The Jewish trio were a great comfort to Paul. "Comfort" (Gk, *parēgorikos*) occurs only here in the New Testament.

Epaphras is described as "one of you" (v. 12). He also sends a greeting to the Colossian church in the letter. From among all Paul's fellow workers, MacDonald writes, "Epaphras is perhaps the most important to the Colossians themselves. In 1:6–8 he is

---

8. Moule, *Colossians and Philemon*, 136–37.

9. Abbott, *Ephesians and Colossians*, 300.

10. Moule, *Colossians and Philemon*, 138.

11. O'Brien, *Colossians, Philemon*, 250.

described as the one who delivered the gospel to them." [12] He also prayed constantly for the Christians in Colossae, and this again underlines the importance of prayer. He prayed intensely that they "may never lapse but always hold perfectly and securely to the will of God." Paul uses the word "striving" or "struggling" (Gk, *agōnizomenos*) because, as Bruce comments, "Prayer is work" and requires great effort.[13] Epaphras asks God that the Colossians will "stand mature," or be "fully assured" (i.e. be secure in their faith).

Epaphras is seemingly commended on two grounds: first, for his constant prayer (v. 12); second, for his hard toil (v. 13).[14] His "working tirelessly" may be in prayer or may involve his more general tireless labor. The word means heavy physical work and emotional distress. Epaphras works tirelessly not only for the Colossians, but also for the other churches of the Lycus Valley, including the other two cities of Laodicea and Hierapolis. Hierapolis is six miles from Colossae; Laodicea, an important trade center, is eleven miles away. The three churches worked together, perhaps with Epaphras as superintendent, bishop, or senior pastor.

Luke the beloved physician sends greetings too. This is the Luke traditionally associated with the Gospel. He is mentioned in 2 Tim 4:11 and Phlm 24 (both of which link him with Mark, as does Colossians), and as a companion of Paul in Acts. Robertson writes, "Both Mark and Luke are with Paul at this time, possibly also with of their copies of their Gospels with them."[15] Most scholars would regard Robertson's comment as at best speculative.

Greetings are also sent from Demas (v. 14), whose name is a contraction of Demetrius. In 1 Tim 4:10 he is described as one who deserted Paul because "he loved the world."

Among those Paul picks out by name to receive his greetings is either a woman called Nympha or a man called Nymphas, who hosts a church in Laodicea. As we observed in our textual notes, the name is disputed, but the UBS Committee favored the feminine

12. MacDonald, *Colossians, Ephesians*, 181.

13. Bruce, *Ephesians and Colossians*, 307.

14. Lincoln, *Colossians*, 667.

15. Roberson, *Word Pictures in the New Testament*, vol. 4, 512.

partly because it received the support of B (Vaticanus). Lightfoot argues in detail for the masculine, although this is still speculative.[16] Abbott argues that if it were feminine, the form would be in the Doric dialect, which would be "highly improbable."[17] Understandably the MSS differed correspondingly on the pronoun "her" and "his." And we cannot depend on Greek accents to settle the dispute since they were lacking from the earliest MSS, so the issue cannot be decided with certainty.

This letter would have been read aloud in public in a gathering of the church (v. 16). Paul's intention was that it be read out in more than one congregation in the Lycus Valley, specifying Laodicea as another venue for its reception. He also asks the Colossians to read "the letter from Laodicea" in their own congregation.[18] Many argue that the letter from Laodicea might well have been a circular letter, which we now know as "Ephesians," although John Knox identified it as Philemon.[19] Colossians and Ephesians certainly supplement each other.

Paul also sends a specific message for Archippus (v. 17). This man is mentioned only here and in Philemon 2, where he is mentioned in connection with Philemon and his wife and their house church. The message is: "Attend to the Christian ministry that you have received in the Lord, so that you may discharge it fully." Commentators, however, are unsure what his task was.

The list of names in vv. 7–17 demonstrates Paul's capacity for leading a team. Wesley writes, "The ministry—Not a lordship, but a service; a laborious and painful work; an obligation to do and suffer all things; to be the least, and the servant of all."[20]

Up to this point in the letter Paul has been dictating to an amanuensis. Now in v. 18 he writes as himself, in his own hand, as

16. Lightfoot, *Colossians and Philemon*, 242.

17. Abbott, *Ephesians and Colossians*, 157.

18. Our translation, "have it read" renders the Greek *poiēsate hina*, which means to "cause that" it be read (O'Brien, *Colossians, Philemon*, 257).

19. Knox, *Philemon among the Letters of Paul*, 38–47.

20. Wesley, *Colossians*, 34.

he does in 1 Cor 16:21; Gal 6:11; 2 Thess 3:17; and Phlm 19. This procedure was a common technique in Paul's day.[21]

His final appeal to his audience is that they remember his chains. "Remember" includes remembering in prayer as well as acknowledging or noting. He begs those Christians who are free to remember those who are in prison for the faith. Moulton suggests that by implication the comfortably off might be encouraged to remember the poor, the healthy to remember the sick, and those who are care-free to remember the worried.[22]

"Grace be with you" (Gk, *charis meth' hymōn*) is the briefest conclusion to any of Paul's letters.

Questions for reflection

1. Do we prize the opportunity for face-to-face conversation as sometimes better than an email or written correspondence? Does face-to-face communication sometimes clarify what is said orally?

2. How often do our conversations bring heartfelt encouragement to others? Or are they spoiled by unnecessary negative criticisms?

3. Do we treat former thieves and runaways (like Onesimus) on an equal footing with other Christians?

4. How important is it to pray that fellow Christians will be well grounded in the Christian faith? Do we too easily underrate Christian doctrine?

5. Do we fully appreciate the prayer and work carried out for us by pastors, overseers, and other Christians?

6. Does our local church work closely with other churches in our neighborhood? Do we encourage networking?

21. Deissmann, *Light from the Ancient East*, 159–60.
22. Moulton, *Colossians, Philemon, and Ephesians*, 68.

7. Do our prayers seek new opportunities for the gospel? Do we pray earnestly?

8. What can we learn from Mark, Onesimus, and Demas about overcoming our failures? Are these lessons very different?

Bibliography

Abbott, Thomas K. *A Critical and Exegetical Commentary on the Epistles to the Ephesians and to the Colossians.* ICC. Edinburgh: T. & T. Clark, 1897.

Balz, H., and Schneider, G., eds. *Exegetical Dictionary of the New Testament.* 3 Vols. Grand Rapids: Eerdmans, 1990–93.

Barr, James. *The Semantics of Biblical Language.* Oxford: Oxford University Press, 1961.

Bartchy, S. Scott. *"Mallon chrēsai: First Century Slavery and the Interpretation of 1 Corinthians 7:21.* Missoula: Scholars, 1973.

Bauckham, Richard. *God Crucified: Monotheism and Christology in the New Testament.* Carlisle, UK: Paternoster, 1998.

———. "Where Is Wisdom to be Found? (Colossians 1:15–20)." In *Reading Texts, Seeking Wisdom: Scripture and Theology,* edited by David F. Ford and Graham N. Stanton, 129–38. London: SCM, 2003.

Bedale, S. F. B. "The Meaning of *kephalē* in the Pauline Epistles." *Journal of Theological Studies* 5 (1954) 211–15.

Behm, Johannes. *"Kardia* in the New Testament." In *TDNT,* vol. 3, 605–14.

Bertram, Georg. *"ōdin"* (woes). In *TDNT,* vol. 9, 671–73.

Bjerkelund, C. J. *Parakalō: Form, Funktion und Sinn der parakalō-Sätze in den paulinischen Briefe.* Oslo: Universitetsforlaget, 1967.

Bornkamm, G. "The Heresy of Colossians." In *Conflict at Colossae,* edited by F. O. Francis and W. A. Meeks, 123–45. Missoula: Scholars, 1973.

Brown, F., S. R. Driver, and C. A. Briggs. *The New BDB Hebrew and English Lexicon.* Lafayette: Associated Publishers, 1980.

Bruce, F. F., with E. K. Simpson. *The Epistles of Paul to the Ephesians and to the Colossians.* NLC. London: Marshall, 1957.

Burney, C. F. "Christ as the *Archē* of Creation." *Journal of Theological Studies* 27 (1926) 160–77.

Caird, George B. "The Glory of God in the Fourth Gospel: An Exercise in Biblical Semantics." *New Testament Studies* 15 (1969) 265–77.

———. *Paul's Letters from Prison.* Oxford: Oxford University Press, 1976.

Calvin, John. *Commentaries on the Epistles to the Philippians, Colossians, and Thessalonians.* Grand Rapids: Eerdmans, 1957.

Cannon, George E. *The Use of Traditional Materials in Colossians*. Macon, GA: Mercer, 1983.

Carrington, Philip. *The Primitive Christian Catechism*. Cambridge: Cambridge University Press, 1940.

Chrysostom, John. *Homilies on the Epistle to the Colossians*. In *Nicene and Post Nicene Fathers*, vol. 13, 257–321. Reprint, Peabody, MA: Hendrickson, 1994.

————. *Homilies on Epistle to the Corinthians*. In *Nicene and Post Nicene Fathers*, vol. 12, 3–270. Reprint, Peabody, MA: Hendrickson, 1994.

Collins, John N. *Diakonia: Re-Interpreting the Sources*. 1990. Reprint, Oxford: Oxford University Press, 2009.

Crafton, Jeffrey A. *The Agency of the Apostle: A Dramatistic Analysis of Paul's Responses to Conflict in 2 Corinthians*. JSNTS 51. Sheffield: JSNTS, 1991.

Croft, Stephen. *Ministry in Three Dimensions: Ordination and Leadership in the Local Church*. London: DLT, 1999.

Danker, Frederick W. *A Greek-English Lexicon of the New Testament and Other Early Christian Literature*. BDAG. 3rd ed. Chicago: Chicago University Press, 2000.

Davies, W. D. *Paul and Rabbinic Judaism*. London: SPCK, 1958.

Deissmann, Adolf. *Bible Studies*. ET. Edinburgh: T. & T. Clark, 1909.

————. *Light from the Ancient East*. ET. London: Hodder, 1927.

Denney, James. *The Death of Christ: Its Place and Interpretation in the New Testament*. London: Hodder and Stoughton, 1922.

Duncan, George S. *St. Paul's Ephesian Ministry: A Reconstruction*. London: Hodder, 1929

Dunn, J. D. G. *The Epistles to the Colossians and to Philemon*. NIGTC. Grand Rapids: Eerdmans, 1996.

————. *Unity and Diversity in the New Testament*. 2nd ed. London: SCM, 1990.

Fletcher-Louis, Crispin. *Jesus Monotheism: Christological Origins: The Emerging Consensus and Beyond*. Eugene, OR: Cascade, 2015.

Gordley, Matthew E. *The Colossian Hymn in Context: An Exegesis in Light of Jewish and Greco-Roman Hymnic and Epistolary Conventions*. WUNT 2, 228. Tübingen: Mohr, 2007.

————. *Teaching through Song in Antiquity: Didactic Hymnody among Greeks, Romans, Jews, and Christians*. WUNT 2, 302. Tübingen: Mohr, 2011.

Gundry, Robert H. *Sōma in Biblical Theology with Emphasis on Pauline Anthropology*. SNTSMS 29. Cambridge: Cambridge University Press, 1976.

Hammerton-Kelly, R. G. *Pre-existence, Wisdom, and the Son of Man*. Cambridge: Cambridge University Press, 1973.

Hanson, Anthony T. *Studies in Paul's Technique and Theology*. London: SPCK, 1974.

Harris, Murray J. *Colossians and Philemon*. Grand Rapids: Eerdmans, 1991.

Hooker, Morna D. "Were There False Teachers in Colossae?" In *Christ and Spirit in the New Testament*, edited by Barnabas Lindars and Stephen S. Smalley,

315–31. Cambridge: Cambridge University Press, 1973. (Reprinted in M. D. Hooker, *From Adam to Christ: Essays on Paul*, 121–36. Cambridge: Cambridge University Press, 1990.)

Hübner, H. "*Plērōma*." In *Exegetical Dictionary of the New Testament*, vol. 3, edited by H. Balz and G. Schneider, 110–11. 3 Vols. Grand Rapids: Eerdmans, 1990–93.

Hunter, A. M. *Paul and His Predecessors*. 2nd ed. London: SCM, 1961.

Hurtado, Larry W. *Lord Jesus Christ: Devotion to Jesus in Earliest Christianity*. Grand Rapids: Eerdmans, 2003.

———. *One God, One Lord: Christian Devotion and Ancient Jewish Monotheism*. Grand Rapids: Eerdmans, 2005.

Jewett, Robert. *Paul's Anthropological Terms: A Study of Their Use in Conflict Settings*. Leiden: Brill, 1971.

Kähler, Else. *Die Frau in den paulinischen Briefen*. Zürich: Benziger, 1960.

Käsemann, Ernst. "A Primitive Christian Baptismal Liturgy." In *Essays on New Testament Themes*, 149–68. ET. London: SCM, 1964.

Keesmaat, Sylvia C. "Colossians." In *Dictionary for Theological Interpretation of the Bible*, edited by in Kevin J. Vanhoozer et al., 119–23. Grand Rapids: Baker Academic, 2005.

Knox, John. *Philemon among the Letters of Paul*. London: Collins, 1960.

Kremer, Jacob. "Was an den Bedrängnissen des Christus Mangelt: Versucht einer bibeltheologischen Neuinterpretatation von Kol. 1:24." *Biblica* 82 (2001) 130–46.

Kümmel, Werner G. *Introduction to the New Testament*. ET. London: SCM, 1963.

Lightfoot, J. B. *St. Paul's Epistles to the Colossians and to Philemon: A Revised Text with Introductions, Notes, and Dissertations*. London: MacMillan, 1876.

Lincoln, Andrew T. *The Letter to the Colossians: Introduction, Commentary, and Reflections*. In *The New Interpreter's Bible*, vol. 11, 551–669. Nashville: Abingdon, 2000.

Lohse, Eduard. *Colossians and Philemon: A Commentary on the Epistles to the Colossians and to Philemon*. ET. Hermeneia. Philadelphia: Fortress, 1971.

Lohse, Eduard. "Christusherrschaft und Kirche im Kolosserbrief." *New Testament Studies* 11 (1964–65) 203–16.

Lossky, Vladimir. *In the Image and Likeness of God*. London: Mowbray, 1974.

———. *The Mystical Theology of the Eastern Church*. New York: St Vladimir's Seminary Press, 1976.

MacDonald, Margaret Y. *Colossians, Ephesians*. Sacra Pagina. 2000. Reprint, Collegeville, MN: Liturgical, 2008.

Martin, Dale B. *Slavery as Salvation*. New Haven, CT: Yale University Press, 1990.

Martin, Ralph P. *Carmen Christi: Philippians 2:5–11 in Recent Interpretation and in the Setting of Early Christian Worship*. SNTSMS 4. Cambridge: Cambridge University Press, 1967.

———. *Colossians and Philemon.* NCB. London: Oliphants, 1978.

McKnight, Scot. *The Letter to the Colossians.* NIC. Grand Rapids: Eerdmans, 2018.

Metzger, Bruce M. *A Textual Commentary on the Greek New Testament.* Stuttgart: UBS, 1994.

Moo, Douglas J. *The Letters to the Colossians and to Philemon.* PNTC. Grand Rapids: Eerdmans, 2008.

Moule, C. F. D. *The Epistles to the Colossians and to Philemon.* CGTC. Cambridge: Cambridge University Press, 1962.

Moulton, Harold K. *Colossians, Philemon, and Ephesians.* London: Epworth, 1963.

Moulton, J. H., and G. Milligan. *Vocabulary of the New Testament.* London: Hodder, 1952.

Norden, E. *Agnostos Theos.* 4th ed. Darmstadt: Wissenschaftliche Buchgesellschaft, 1956.

O'Brien, Peter T. *Colossians, Philemon.* WBC. Nashville: Nelson, 1982.

Ogg, George. *The Chronology of the Life of Paul.* London: Epworth, 1968.

Pao, David W. *Colossians and Philemon.* ECNT. Grand Rapids: Zondervan, 2012.

Peake, A. S. *Colossians.* In *The Expositor's Greek Testament,* vol. 3, edited by W. Robertson Nicoll, 477–547. 1917. Reprint, Grand Rapids: Eerdmans, 1956.

Pfitzner, Victor C. *Paul and the Agon Motif: Traditional Athletic Imagery in Pauline Literature.* ; Novum Testamentum Supplement. Leiden: Brill, 1967.

Polhill, J. B. "The Relationship between Ephesians and Colossians." *Review and Expositor* 70 (1973) 439–50.

Reitzenstein, R. *Hellenistic Mystery Religions: Their Basic Ideas and Significance.* Pittsburgh: Pickwick, 1978.

Rengstorf, Karl H. "*Doulos,* slave." In *TDNT,* vol. 2, 270–73.

Richards, E. Randolph. *Paul and First-Century Letter Writing: Secretaries, Composition and Collection.* Downers Grove, IL: IVP Academic, 2004.

Richards, E. Randolph. *The Secretary in the Letters of Paul.* WUNT2/42. Tübingen: Mohr/Siebeck, 1991.

Robertson, Archibald T. *Word Pictures in the New Testament,* vol. 4. New York: Smith, 1931.

Robinson, James M. "A Formal Analysis of Colossians 1:15–20." *Journal of Biblical Literature* 76 (1957) 270–87.

Robinson, John A. T. *The Body.* London: SCM, 1952.

Sanders, E. P. *Paul and Palestinian Judaism.* London: SCM, 1977.

Schweizer, Eduard. "Slaves of the Elements and Worshipers of Angels: Gal. 4:3, 9 and Col. 2:8, 18, 20." *JBL* 107 (1988) 455–68.

———. "*sōma*" ("body" in Colossians). In *TDNT,* vol. 7, 1074–77.

Schubert, Paul. *Form and Function of Pauline Thanksgivings.* Berlin: Mohr, 1959.

Scott, Ernest F. *The Epistles of Paul to the Colossians, to Philemon, and to the Ephesians.* London: Hodder & Stoughton, 1930.

Selwyn, E. G. *The First Epistle of St Peter.* London: MacMillan, 1946.

Settler, Hanna. "An Interpretation of Colossians 1:24 in the Framework of Paul's Mission." In *The Mission of the Early Church to Jews and Gentiles,* edited by Jostein Adna and Hans Kvalbein, 187–89. WUNT, 127. Tübingen: Mohr, 2000.

Smith, Ian K. *Heavenly Perspective: A Study of the Apostle Paul's Response to a Jewish Mystical Element at Colossae.* London: T. & T. Clark, 2006.

Strack, Hermann L., and Paul Billerbeck. *Kommentar zum Neuen Testament aus Talmud und Midrasch.* 3 vols. Munich: Beck, 1969.

Synge, F. C. *Philippians and Colossians.* London: SCM, 1951.

Thiselton, Anthony C. *The First Epistle to the Corinthians.* NIGTC. Grand Rapids: Eerdmans, 2000.

———. *Life after Death: A New Approach to the Last Things.* Grand Rapids: Eerdmans, 2012.

Thompson, Marianne Meye. *Colossians and Philemon.* NH. Grand Rapids: Eerdmans, 2005.

Thornton, Lionel S. *The Common Life in the Body of Christ.* London: Dacre, 1944.

Wesley, John. *Colossians: Explanatory Notes and Commentary.* London: Hargreaves, 1755.

White, R. E. O. *Colossians.* In *The Broadman Commentary* vol. 11, 217–56. London: Broadman, 1971.

Williamson, L. "Led in Triumph: Paul's Use of *Thriambeuō*." *Interpretation* 22 (1968) 317–32.

Wilson, Robert McLachlan. *A Critical and Exegetical Commentary on Colossians and Philemon.* ICC. London: Bloomsbury/T. & T. Clark, 2005.

Wright, N. T. *Colossians and Philemon.* TNTC. Leicester, UK: IVP, 1986.

———. "Poetry and Theology in Colossians 1:15–20." *New Testament Studies* 36.3 (1990) 444–68.

Index of Names

Index of Subjects

Index of Biblical References

INDEX OF BIBLICAL REFERENCES